CORPORATE ATHLETES!

YOU ARE THE PLAYER, YOU ARE THE CAPTAIN, YOU ARE THE COACH

Kishore Kumar Thakur

Clever Fox®
PUBLISHING
Chennai • Bangalore

CLEVER FOX PUBLISHING
Chennai, India

Published by CLEVER FOX PUBLISHING 2025

ISBN: 978-93-7500-061-7

Dedication

To every professional who chooses **awareness over ambition, growth over comfort,** *and* **purpose over pressure.**

To those who show up each day — not just to meet targets, but to make a difference.

To the ones who pause to reflect, who lead with empathy, and who coach with belief.

You are the true **Corporate Athletes** *— playing the inner game with courage, the outer game with excellence, and the human game with heart.*

CONTENTS

FOREWORD

By Dr. V. Vijayalakshmi, Faculty - Department of Management Studies, IIT Madras

In the evolving landscape of work, where boundaries blur and demands intensify, the metaphor of the "Corporate Athlete" emerges as both timely and transformative. This book by Kishore Kumar Thakur reframes the very essence of how professionals can sustain excellence while preserving purpose. Written with clarity and conviction, it invites readers to see themselves not as passive participants in organizational life, but as active players in a lifelong sport of mastery.

The concept of the Corporate Athlete is not new in spirit, yet rarely has it been articulated with such precision and accessibility. By drawing parallels between the discipline of world-class athletes and the realities of corporate professionals, the author bridges two domains that often remain disconnected -Sports and Management. Athletes train, recover, and renew before stepping into competition. Professionals, by contrast, are expected to perform continuously, with little rehearsal and even less reflection. This book challenges that paradox, offering a framework where rhythm replaces exhaustion, and energy becomes the true currency of performance.

Readers will find themselves guided through a journey that is both intellectual and experiential. The narrative is grounded in psychology, coaching science, and leadership practice, yet it is enriched with stories of athletes such as Neeraj Chopra, P.V. Sindhu, and M.S. Dhoni; figures whose resilience and composure under pressure throw light upon the lessons for boardrooms and business units alike. These stories are woven into the fabric of corporate life, reminding professionals that the principles of recovery, rhythm, and renewal are as relevant in the workplace as they are on the playing field.

What distinguishes this work is its insistence on balance. The book does not glorify relentless ambition or unbroken intensity. Instead, it underscores the hidden costs of high performance; burnout, fatigue, and disconnection from purpose. In doing so, it offers a corrective lens: success is not defined by output alone, but by sustainable excellence. The Corporate Athlete framework, embodying the roles of Player, Captain, and Coach, provides a practical yet profound model for professionals to integrate discipline, leadership, and reflection into their daily rhythm.

The impact of this book extends beyond corporate corridors. Its insights resonate with educators, leaders, and anyone navigating the pressures of modern life. The emphasis on energy mastery over time management, on renewal as a strategic necessity rather than a luxury, and on purpose as the anchor of performance, makes it universally relevant. It is a playbook to be lived.

The author's synthesis of coaching principles from the International Coaching Federation and the European Mentoring and Coaching Council lends credibility, while his integration of lived corporate experiences ensures relevance. Yet the book is not academic in the restrictive sense; it is a practitioner's reflection, shaped by years of coaching, observation, and dialogue. Its strength lies in its ability to translate theory into practice, and practice into wisdom.

For the corporate audience, the book offers a mirror. It reflects the pressures of deadlines, the fatigue of constant performance, and the silent erosion of purpose. For the broader audience, it offers an invitation: to see work not as a race to win, but as an infinite game where mastery and meaning converge.

In endorsing this work, one cannot help but acknowledge its dual impact. It informs, but it also transforms. It provides frameworks, but it also provokes reflection. It speaks to organizations, but it also speaks to individuals. Above all, it reminds readers that excellence is not achieved by doing more, but by aligning effort with energy, and ambition with awareness.

This book deserves to be read slowly, lived deliberately, and revisited often. I had to pause in several places because the ideas are deeply resonant. It is a companion for professionals seeking to perform with excellence, lead with vision, and coach with empathy. It is also a reminder that in the end, the greatest victories are not those measured by metrics, but those sustained by rhythm, resilience, and renewal.

The Corporate Athlete is a mindset, a practice, and a way of being. Kishore Thakur has given professionals a language for what they have long felt but rarely articulated: that success without well-being is survival, and that true mastery lies in balancing the inner game with the outer one.

This foreword, written in recognition of the book's significance, affirms its place as a vital contribution to the literature on performance and leadership. It is offered with respect for the author's vision, and with confidence that readers will find in these pages not only insights, but also inspiration to play their own infinite game with courage, clarity, and heart. I use Sports analogies while facilitating / teaching courses on Organizational Behavior here at IIT Madras. I am excited to use some of the examples provided in this book in my upcoming classes.

FOREWORD

By Bernd Knobloch, Director at Deutsche Bank

In a world that emphasizes constant motion, where professionals are urged to deliver more, faster, and better, Corporate Athletes! offers a rare and necessary pause. It invites us to rethink performance — not as an endless sprint toward external success, but as a disciplined, conscious pursuit of inner mastery.

This is not another book about productivity or leadership clichés. It's a deeply reflective playbook that bridges the science of performance with the art of self-awareness. Through the powerful metaphor of the athlete, Kishore reframes how we see ourselves at work — not merely as performers chasing outcomes, but as evolving beings training for endurance, purpose, and growth.

The Corporate Athlete Framework — with its roles of the Player, the Captain, and the Coach — is both elegant and transformative. It reminds us that excellence begins with self-leadership, matures through compassionate influence, and culminates in empowering others. The integration of sports psychology, leadership science, and coaching wisdom gives this book both rigor and heart.

I myself have worked with Kishore to reframe how I had previously thought about my own leadership practice and have benefited from his guidance, encouragement and insight. Along the way, his coaching has touched many of the central themes conceptualized in the Corporate Athlete framework. It has helped me to sharpen my focus and gain clarity on what performance and leadership in a corporate environment really means.

What I appreciate most is its emphasis on balance — on managing energy, not just time; on recovery as a strategic advantage, not a luxury. In drawing lessons from championship athletes, Corporate Athletes! reveals that what separates the great from the good is not only skill or strategy, but mindset and meaning.

For professionals striving to lead with resilience and authenticity, this book is more than a guide. It challenges us to slow down, to reflect, and to rediscover the joy of playing the long game.

As you turn these pages, prepare not just to learn, but to transform how you show up — for yourself, your teams, and your purpose. Because as Corporate Athletes! so powerfully reminds us, true leadership isn't about doing more; it's about being more.

It's been a privilege to witness this framework come alive — not just as a model, but as a mindset that truly transforms the way we lead.

FOREWORD

By James D Glover, Sr. Director Product Management

The book Corporate Athletes! by Kishore Kumar Thakur proposes a powerful new mindset for professionals—one that shifts from the traditional employee model to the identity of a *Corporate Athlete*. The workplace, Kishore argues, has become an arena with pressures and demands not unlike a sports stadium. And just as athletes must train, recover, and reflect to achieve sustained excellence, professionals too must learn to manage their **energy**, not just their time. This fresh paradigm invites readers to balance performance with purpose and move from merely surviving to truly thriving in their careers.

As a Silicon Valley professional, I relate deeply to these ideas. Over twenty years in product management has allowed me to observe how every part of an organization—engineering, manufacturing, supply chain, sales, marketing, support—requires people to play different roles. Kishore's framework of **Player, Captain, and Coach** applies to each of these domains and many more.

You may be wondering about the person behind this Corporate Athlete concept. Kishore Kumar Thakur is an accredited **Professional Certified Coach (PCC)** with the International

Coach Federation (ICF). He specializes in **Personal Growth, Inner Peace, and Professional Development**, and has coached more than **800 leaders** across start-ups, mid-size businesses, and major global brands. His client list includes leaders from Apple, Google, Facebook, Deloitte, American Express, IBM, Salesforce, AB InBev, MRF, and the Indian School of Business. Through his transformational, neuroscience-based approach, he helps professionals create deep and lasting change at a subconscious level, enabling them to perform at their highest potential.

I first met Kishore several years ago as a coaching client—and I remain one today. Many of the principles in this book were shared with me directly. Kishore helped me understand how the Corporate Athlete model applied to my situation, offering both clarity and direction. Together, we built a personal career vision aligned with my goals, strengths, and values.

As a longtime admirer of Stephen Covey, I was once convinced that **time management** was the ultimate key to professional success. Time management involves planning, prioritizing, organizing, and making conscious decisions about how to focus one's efforts. And while those skills remain valuable, Kishore introduces a deeper truth: human beings are emotional, imperfect, and cannot perform at optimal levels every hour of every day.

Kishore emphasizes that **energy management**—not time management—is the real foundation of sustainable success. He writes, *"Unlike athletes who train, rest, and renew, most professionals are expected to perform continuously — often at the cost of energy, focus, and well-being."* Self-awareness plays a crucial role in building a personal energy blueprint that supports resilience and high performance.

A central theme of the book is energy across four dimensions: **physical, emotional, mental, and spiritual**. Time is finite, but energy can be renewed. Through small, consistent habits and recovery practices, professionals can replenish their energy reserves and avoid burnout—a widespread challenge in today's workplaces.

This book serves as an engaging and practical playbook for anyone seeking a healthier, more intentional path to professional excellence. It encourages readers to embrace continuous improvement, to see reflection and recovery as essential—not optional—and to take ownership of their career journey. By highlighting purpose, inner strength, and small, consistent actions, Kishore provides a compelling roadmap for long-term fulfillment and peak performance.

If you wish to engage the world as a **Corporate Athlete**, consider this book your personal playbook. Take the time to answer its questions thoughtfully, and revisit them often. Just as an athlete does not read the playbook once, neither should you. As you grow, your understanding will expand, and your goals will evolve.

The principles in this book have helped me reach new levels of clarity, success, and satisfaction in my career. I hope they do the same for you.

– James Glover

FOREWORD

By Suresh Ramamurthi, People Development Coach

In the world of sports, greatness is often defined by moments of brilliance—an electrifying sprint, a game-winning shot, a record shattered. Athletes train relentlessly, push their limits, and inspire millions. Yet when injury strikes or fatigue sets in, they are given the space to pause, recover, and return—renewed, focused, and stronger than before.

In the corporate arena, however, the professional rarely enjoys that luxury. There are no timeouts, no injury breaks, no off-seasons. The corporate athlete must hit the ground running and stay in the race every single day. Any pause risks losing the edge, any lapse demands a climb back to peak performance.

This book draws a compelling parallel between these two high-performance worlds—sports and business—and redefines professionals as *corporate athletes*: individuals in a constant pursuit of excellence, growth, and mastery.

The author introduces a vital paradigm shift—from **time management** to **energy management**—where energy is explored across four dimensions: **physical, emotional, mental, and spiritual**. It's a powerful reminder that sustained performance isn't about pushing harder, but about managing one's energy wisely. Constant exertion without renewal leads to burnout; strategic recovery restores vitality and clarity.

What makes this narrative so powerful is its recognition of the corporate leader as a multidimensional force—**strategist, motivator, mentor, and performer**—often without the freedom to recover or reflect that a sportsperson enjoys. Just as a coach shapes a team's destiny, the corporate leader must cultivate talent, drive results, and navigate change—all while maintaining their own equilibrium and purpose.

Having personally experienced the pressures of corporate life, played many of the roles described in this book, and observed closely what athletes endure in their careers, I can attest that this comparison is striking—and the insights, profound. *Corporate Athlete* doesn't just compare these worlds; it elevates our understanding of what leadership means in the modern age.

It invites us to reimagine leadership through the lens of **energy, adaptability, and emotional intelligence**. It urges every professional to see themselves not merely as a participant in the corporate game—but as the player, the captain, and the coach of their own performance.

To every leader who performs without pause, who coaches without a whistle, and who leads without applause—this book is for you.

– Suresh Ramamurthi,
People Development Coach

ACKNOWLEDGMENTS

Every book is a team effort, even when it appears to have a single author's name on the cover.

"Corporate Athletes! You are the Player, you are the Captain, you are the Coach" is no exception. It is the result of years of conversations, coaching sessions, observations, and quiet reflections — shaped by the wisdom and generosity of many people.

To the many professionals, leaders, and teams I have had the privilege to coach — thank you for trusting me with your stories, your challenges, and your aspirations. Each conversation taught me something new about courage, resilience, and the human capacity to grow. You are the true inspiration behind this book.

To my mentors and teachers in the coaching and leadership community — your insights into human potential and your commitment to continuous learning have deeply influenced my own philosophy. The frameworks and reflections in this book stand on the strong foundations of your wisdom and example.

To my colleagues, clients, and friends from across organizations and industries — thank you for being part of this journey of experimentation and evolution. Your feedback, encouragement, and curiosity have helped refine these ideas into practical tools for growth and leadership.

To my family — thank you for your patience and unconditional support. For understanding the long writing hours, the quiet moments of reflection, and the countless drafts that turned into this book. Your belief in me has been my constant source of strength and balance.

To my early readers and well-wishers who reviewed drafts and offered thoughtful perspectives — your encouragement pushed me to go deeper, write clearer, and connect more authentically. This book carries your fingerprints in its pages.

Finally, to the readers — thank you for choosing to spend your time with these ideas. If this book helps you pause, reflect, and play your own game with more purpose and presence, then it has fulfilled its mission.

Because, in the end, this is not just my book — it is *our* shared journey toward awareness, excellence, and renewal.
With gratitude and respect,

– Kishore Kumar Thakur

AUTHOR'S NOTE

On Sources, Inspirations, and Learning

The ideas, frameworks, and reflections shared in this book are not mine alone. They are a synthesis of insights gathered over years of learning, observing, reflecting, and coaching.

Every page carries echoes of real corporate experiences and human stories — drawn from leaders, colleagues, mentors, and clients who shaped my understanding of what it means to perform, lead, and grow with awareness.

While I have drawn inspiration from the disciplines of ***sport, psychology, and leadership****, my references to athletes and sports metaphors are based on publicly known stories, research, and observation — not personal association. They serve as mirrors, helping us see the parallels between the playing field and the workplace.*

Much of this work is informed by coaching principles and frameworks established by the ***International Coaching Federation (ICF)*** *and the* ***European Mentoring and Coaching Council (EMCC)****. The interpretations, integrations, and expressions presented here, however, are entirely my own — shaped through practice, reflection, and real-world experience.*

This book is not an academic text, but a practitioner's reflection — a synthesis of insights gathered from working with professionals who strive daily to balance performance, leadership, and purpose.

If any idea here resonates with you, the credit belongs to the teachers, thinkers, and coaches who continue to illuminate this shared journey. If something feels incomplete, it simply reflects my own evolution — because growth, like excellence, is always a work in progress.

My intention is not to claim expertise, but to contribute — to add a small voice to the larger conversation about how we can work, lead, and live with greater meaning and mastery.

– Kishore Thakur

INTRODUCTION / PREFACE

Corporate Athletes!

You are the Player. You are the Captain. You are the Coach.

When I first began working in the corporate world, I believed success was about doing more — working harder, learning faster, and staying ahead.

But over the years, I began noticing something deeper. Even the most talented professionals — those who gave everything to their careers — were often running on empty. They were high-performing, but low-renewal. They were sprinting hard, but not always in the right direction.

As a coach, I've seen this pattern across boardrooms and business units — individuals performing at full capacity, yet quietly losing connection with their purpose, joy, or sense of self. That's when I began to see the parallel: corporate professionals are a lot like athletes.

The Corporate Arena

Think about it. Every day, professionals walk into their own version of the arena — boardrooms, client calls, reviews, deadlines. They face pressure, competition, uncertainty, and constant change.

Deadlines become finish lines. Projects become tournaments. And burnout — that's our version of injury time.

But here's the difference. Athletes train before they compete. They have coaches, recovery rituals, and systems that protect their performance. Corporate professionals often don't. They are expected to perform every day, with little time for reflection or renewal.

It's like being in a championship match with no timeouts — always on, rarely recovering.

That realization became the spark behind this book.

The Birth of the Corporate Athlete

What if we approached our work like athletes approach their sport? What if we managed our *energy*, not just our *time*? What if we practiced recovery, reflection, and renewal with the same commitment as we pursue performance?

That's where the idea of the **Corporate Athlete** was born.

A Corporate Athlete is not someone who works harder, but someone who works *consciously* — balancing *performance with purpose*. It's about learning to shift from surviving → thriving → driving — performing at your best, leading with heart, and renewing your energy to sustain excellence.

Every professional plays three roles every day:

1. **The Player** — who performs with focus, skill, and discipline.

2. **The Captain** — who leads with vision, courage, and empathy.
3. **The Coach** — who grows self and others through awareness and reflection.

The Inner Game

The outer game of success is what the world sees — goals, targets, achievements. But the inner game — mindset, energy, resilience, purpose — determines whether that success can be sustained.

Athletes train for both. They visualize, rest, and renew as much as they practice. Likewise, professionals must learn to balance intensity with reflection, and output with inner alignment. That is where coaching becomes the bridge between performance and presence.

When we learn to coach ourselves — to pause, reflect, and realign — we stop running on autopilot and start leading from awareness.

Why This Book Now

The workplace is evolving faster than ever — hybrid models, AI disruption, blurred work-life boundaries, and constant change. Traditional management models rooted in control are giving way to conscious leadership — built on clarity, compassion, and curiosity.

This book invites you to see your work not as a race to win, but as a lifelong sport of mastery and meaning. It's not about chasing success; it's about becoming the kind of person success naturally follows.

What You Will Discover

This is not a theoretical book. It's a playbook — drawing from:

- Lessons from world-class athletes and performance psychology
- Real coaching experiences from corporate life
- Frameworks for energy, purpose, and growth
- Reflective practices that help you apply insights immediately

---

You will learn to:

- **Perform like a Player**, mastering energy and discipline
- **Lead like a Captain**, inspiring with vision and courage
- **Coach like a Leader**, nurturing growth and potential in others

---

A Personal Note

This book is born out of lived experience — of working inside organizations, leading teams, and later coaching leaders across industries.

Over time, I've realized that transformation begins the moment we stop asking, "What's wrong with me?" and start asking, "What's possible for me?"

If this book helps you pause, reflect, and play your game with greater awareness and purpose, then it has done its job.

Because at the end of the day — You are the Player who performs. You are the Captain who leads. You are the Coach who transforms.

And together, you are the Corporate Athlete — the one who performs with purpose, leads with vision, and renews with awareness.

The game is yours. Play it with mastery.

– Kishore Kumar Thakur

Reader's Promise

This book is not meant to be read — it's meant to be *lived.*

As you turn these pages, pause often. Reflect honestly. Try one new practice, one new pause, one new way of seeing yourself at work.

You don't need to rush or agree with every idea. You only need to stay curious.

Because growth doesn't happen through information — it happens through awareness. And awareness, practiced daily, becomes mastery.

If you finish this book feeling more grounded, more conscious, and more connected to your purpose — then the real performance has already begun.

That's the promise — between you, this book, and your best self.

– Kishore Kumar Thakur

Chapter 1

THE NEW GAME OF WORK: ENTERING THE ARENA OF THE CORPORATE ATHLETE

"The difference between good and great is not talent—it's how you train when no one is watching."

– M.S. Dhoni

The Arena Has Changed

The modern workplace no longer resembles the predictable office of the 1990s. It has morphed into a **performance arena**—alive with movement, metrics, and momentum.

Each email, each presentation, each meeting is a mini-match where expectations run high and applause is silent. You walk into work like an athlete entering a stadium, carrying unseen gear: your laptop, your mindset, your energy.

The crowd may not be cheering, but the pressure is real. And unlike traditional athletes who have time to train, corporate athletes perform **every single day** with little rehearsal and even less recovery.

Neeraj Chopra — Rhythm Under Pressure

On an August evening in 2021, Neeraj Chopra stood poised for his javelin throw at the Tokyo Olympics. A billion hopes leaned in. His earlier throws were strong, but gold hung in the balance.

He closed his eyes—not in fear, but in focus. Later, he said, "In that moment, I wasn't thinking of the medal. I was thinking of rhythm."

That word—**rhythm**—is what separates exhaustion from excellence. Each athlete knows: pressure is inevitable, but burnout is optional when rhythm is right.

When Neeraj's javelin flew, it carried years of disciplined cycles—training, recovery, coaching feedback, self-belief. He wasn't merely throwing for distance; he was expressing alignment—mind, body, breath, and purpose moving as one.

The Corporate Parallel: Performing Without Practice

Meet Riya, a senior manager in a global analytics firm. Her day starts before sunrise, pinged by overnight messages. She powers through meetings, decisions, and deadlines—no breaks, no breath.

By evening, she's drained, yet her calendar says "tomorrow: repeat." If Neeraj trains for months to perform for minutes, Riya performs for months without training at all.

That is the corporate paradox: endless performance, minimal preparation. Professionals chase productivity as athletes chase medals, but without rhythm, both risk injury—one physical, the other emotional.

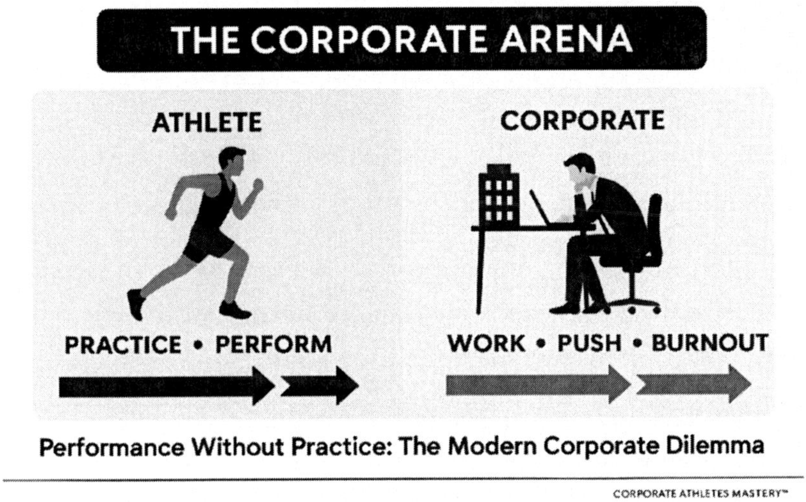

Figure 1: The Corporate Arena — Performance Without Practice

Unlike athletes who train, rest, and renew, most professionals are expected to perform continuously — often at the cost of energy, focus, and well-being

The Hidden Cost of High Performance

For years, the corporate world has celebrated one kind of hero — the high performer. The one who stays late, answers emails at midnight, and never misses a deadline. The one who is "always on," driven, reliable, and seemingly unstoppable.

But behind the polished dashboards and glowing reviews, there is another story — a quieter one that doesn't make it into quarterly reports. It's the story of exhaustion disguised as dedication. Of professionals performing at their peak while silently running on empty.

In the sports world, no athlete would train without recovery. They know that the body and mind need rhythm — effort, pause, renewal, repeat. A runner doesn't sprint through every lap. A cricketer doesn't bat all day without breaks. They respect recovery as much as performance, because they know one fuels the other.

But in the corporate world, recovery is often seen as weakness. Rest becomes something we "earn," not something we *need.* And that's where the imbalance begins.

The Modern Marathon

A few years ago, I was coaching a senior manager, let's call her Meera. On paper, she was exceptional — leading multiple teams, consistently outperforming targets, and admired for her dedication. But the moment she sat across from me in her first session, she sighed and said quietly,

"I feel like I'm always running. I'm performing, but I'm tired. I'm leading, but I'm not in control anymore."

Meera didn't have a performance problem. She had an energy problem.

Her schedule was packed, her phone never silent, her sleep inconsistent. She wasn't failing — she was *fatiguing.*

Through coaching, Meera began to understand something powerful: She wasn't playing the game wrong. She was playing the wrong *version* of the game. She was running a marathon as if it were a sprint.

In sports, athletes alternate between training, performance, and recovery. In corporate life, many professionals skip the recovery stage altogether — treating exhaustion as a badge of honor. The result? They perform, but they don't sustain. They achieve, but they don't evolve.

The Silent Burnout

Burnout rarely announces itself dramatically. It arrives slowly — like a fog that blurs clarity and dulls enthusiasm. It starts with small compromises: skipping a meal, missing a workout, working "just one more hour." Soon, rest feels like a luxury, and passion turns into pressure.

The World Health Organization now recognizes burnout as an occupational phenomenon — a state of chronic workplace stress that has not been successfully managed. Symptoms include emotional exhaustion, mental distance from one's job, and reduced professional efficacy.

But you don't need a diagnosis to know when something is off. You can *feel* it — in your energy, in your motivation, in your sense of joy. You're performing well on the outside, but something inside feels disconnected.

That's the hidden cost of high performance: You keep giving until you have nothing left to give.

What Athletes Know That Professionals Forget

In sports, rest is not the opposite of work — it's part of it. Athletes train hard, yes, but they also recover strategically. They understand the science of energy cycles, the value of nutrition, sleep, and mental reset.

They know that recovery is not a reward for performance — it's a requirement for it.

Professionals, on the other hand, often measure success by output rather than insight. We focus on doing more, not being more. We chase results without realizing that energy, not effort, determines how well we perform.

True excellence doesn't come from constant motion. It comes from rhythm — the balance between focus and renewal.

Reflection: Where Is Your Energy Going?

Take a moment to pause and ask yourself:

1. When was the last time I finished a workweek feeling energized rather than drained?
2. Do I treat recovery as a strategic part of performance — or as a luxury?
3. What's one practice that helps me restore — body, mind, or spirit?

If your answers make you pause, that's good. Awareness is the first step toward mastery.

Because in the new game of work, *how* you manage your energy determines *how far* your performance can go. The Corporate Athlete doesn't just perform harder — they perform wiser.

Key Insight

"Burnout doesn't come from doing too much. It comes from doing too little of what restores you."

From Time Management to Energy Mastery

For decades, we were told to manage time. But time is finite. Energy is renewable.

Neeraj's success was not about working longer; it was about **managing energy across four dimensions**—physical, emotional, mental, and spiritual. Corporate athletes need the same playbook.

Energy Dimension	Athletic Parallel	Corporate Application	Renewal Practice
Physical	Strength & stamina	Sleep 7–8 hrs, move hourly, eat mindfully	Short walks, hydration, posture resets
Emotional	Positivity & resilience	Manage mood & relationships	Gratitude journaling, empathy moments

Energy Dimension	Athletic Parallel	Corporate Application	Renewal Practice
Mental	Focus & strategy	Prioritize deep work	90-minute focus blocks, digital detox
Spiritual	Purpose & alignment	Meaning in work	Reflect on impact, connect to values

Neglect one, and performance cracks. Integrate all, and excellence becomes sustainable.

Injuries of the Invisible Kind

Athletes fear injury; professionals normalize burnout. Neeraj's elbow injury in 2019 forced him into reflection:

"Injury teaches humility. It reminds you that progress is not linear."

Corporate injuries are less visible—anxiety disguised as diligence; fatigue masked as commitment.

- **Physical strain:** Late nights, skipped meals.
- **Emotional strain:** Criticism loops, suppressed stress.
- **Mental strain:** Decision fatigue.
- **Spiritual strain:** Purpose erosion.

Recovery isn't weakness—it's wisdom. As Dhoni once said after a long tournament,

"Rest is not stopping the work. It's preparing for the next innings."

P.V. Sindhu — Resilience in Motion

After losing the 2016 Olympic final, P.V. Sindhu was devastated yet composed. Her coach, Gopichand, recalls that she returned to practice within a week. No bitterness, just quiet commitment: "The next time, I'll finish the match."

Three years later, she became World Champion.

Sindhu's story mirrors every professional who faces rejection, restructuring, or missed promotion. The lesson: **the comeback is built in practice, not performance.**

When setbacks occur, professionals can mirror athletes by asking:

- What did I learn?
- What do I need to strengthen?
- Who can coach me through this phase?

The Science of Flow

Psychologist Mihaly Csikszentmihalyi described *flow* as the state where challenge and skill align. Neuroscience shows that flow floods the brain with dopamine, sharpening focus and creativity.

Athletes enter it through rituals—breath, visualization, and pre-performance routines. Professionals can too, through mindfulness and purpose clarity.

Flow = Focus × Meaning × Recovery.

When organizations encourage reflection pauses instead of endless speed, flow replaces fatigue.

Corporate Stories of Renewal

Rohit — The Sales Sprinter

Rohit's team chased quarterly targets like marathons with no finish lines. Introducing 10-minute "energy huddles" changed everything—micro-recovery between sprints. Performance improved 18 %, and attrition dropped.

Anjali — The HR Captain

After introducing "mindful Mondays" — short reflective check-ins — her division's engagement score climbed. People felt seen, not supervised.

These are examples of **corporate rehabilitation**—small changes that rebuild collective stamina.

Leadership Lessons from M.S. Dhoni

Dhoni's calm under pressure isn't a myth—it's a method. He trains for chaos. When asked about his secret, he said:

"You can't control pressure, but you can control preparation."

In boardrooms, the Dhoni mindset translates to:

- Respond, don't react.

- Observe more, speak less.
- Build others' confidence, not dependence.

Dhoni, the captain, also mentors without noise—reminding leaders that **grace is a leadership strategy**.

The Rhythm of Sustainable Performance

Athletic performance cycles follow four stages: **Perform → Recover → Reflect → Refocus.**

Corporate life often ends at "perform." Integrating the other three is how professionals extend careers without exhaustion.

Practical rhythm redesign:

- After big projects, hold a *learning huddle.*
- Plan rest days post-deadline.
- Celebrate progress, not just output.

Introducing the Corporate Athlete Framework

Every professional plays **three roles within**:

Role	Focus	Power Question
The Player	Personal discipline & execution	*Am I showing up at my best each day?*
The Captain	Leadership & influence	*Am I helping others find their best game?*
The Coach	Growth & reflection	*Am I learning and developing through this journey?*

These roles coexist. A professional who performs only as a Player may achieve, but not lead. A Captain without a Coach mindset may command, but not grow. Balance them, and you become a **Corporate Athlete Master**.

Reflection Pause — Your Current Game

Take five minutes. Write freely.

1. When was the last time you felt fully "in flow"?
2. What do you do to recover between high-pressure tasks?
3. Which role dominates you now—Player, Captain, or Coach?
4. Which one needs more attention this month?

Awareness is your first act of coaching yourself.

Mindset Shifts of a Corporate Athlete

Old Paradigm	Corporate Athlete Mindset
Manage time	Master energy
Work hard	Work rhythmically
Seek control	Build clarity
Focus on tasks	Focus on impact
Compete with others	Compete with yesterday's self

Mastery is not intensity—it's consistency aligned with purpose.

Practice — Design Your Morning Ritual

Before opening your inbox:

1. Center: 3 deep breaths to anchor focus.

2. **Visualize:** Picture today's key outcome.
3. **Intend:** Choose a word for the day (Clarity, Calm, Courage).
4. **Prioritize:** Note three actions that matter most.

Repeat for 21 days. It re-wires attention.

The Inner Game and the Outer Game

Tim Gallwey, pioneer of *The Inner Game*, taught that our greatest opponent isn't others—it's internal interference. Athletes silence that inner critic through focus rituals. Professionals can too, by practicing mindful awareness:

"Between stimulus and response, there is a space. In that space lies our freedom." — Viktor Frankl

Cultivate that space; it's your ultimate advantage.

Redefining Success

Success without well-being is just survival. The new metric of excellence is **sustainable performance**—performing at your best, feeling your best, and bringing out the best in others.

Neeraj's gold, Dhoni's composure, Sindhu's resilience—all point to the same truth: You win the outer game only when you master the inner one.

Closing Reflection

Every morning, you enter your arena. You choose how you show up—rushed or ready, reactive or responsive.

You are the Player who disciplines effort, the Captain who inspires trust, and the Coach who cultivates growth.

That trinity is the heart of a Corporate Athlete. Because in the end, the goal is not to work harder—it's to **play the infinite game of purpose and presence.**

KEY TAKEAWAYS

☑ The modern workplace is a performance arena.
☑ Manage energy, not just time.
☑ Build rhythm: Perform → Recover → Reflect → Refocus.
☑ Embody the three roles—Player, Captain, Coach.
☑ Redefine success as sustainable excellence.

"The greatest victories happen quietly—inside the mind that chooses balance over burnout."

Chapter 2

FROM EMPLOYEE TO ATHLETE: MASTERING ENERGY, NOT JUST TIME

"An athlete doesn't wait for the match to prepare — they prepare every day in body, mind, and soul."

The Time Illusion

For decades, professionals have chased the mirage of **time management** — as if rearranging hours could rearrange outcomes. Bookshelves groan under titles promising to "hack your productivity" and "squeeze more out of every minute." And yet, despite better calendars, apps, and automation, exhaustion remains the new normal.

Why? Because **time isn't the real problem — energy is.**

Time is finite. Energy can be renewed.

You can't stretch hours, but you can elevate how you show up within them. That is the core shift — from employee mindset (managing time) to athlete mindset (managing energy).

Imagine two professionals — both have eight hours. One powers through tasks in half-focus, feeling depleted by mid-afternoon. The other flows through the day with vitality and calm presence, finishing strong.

The difference isn't intelligence or workload — it's **energy design**. Like an athlete training for performance peaks, the Corporate Athlete learns to oscillate between focus and recovery, not push endlessly.

As Roger Federer once said, "Rest is part of the work. Without it, the work suffers."

P.V. Sindhu's Rhythm of Resilience

When P.V. Sindhu lost the 2016 Olympic badminton final to Carolina Marin, she didn't sulk. She smiled. She hugged her opponent. She stood tall.

Her coach, Pullela Gopichand, later shared that she was back on court within a week — training harder, sharper, smarter. There was no drama, only **discipline**.

Sindhu understood something profound: **Defeat is feedback. Fatigue is data. Energy is intelligence.**

She didn't ask, "Why me?" She asked, "What can I learn?" That question transformed her from a finalist into a world champion.

In 2019, when Sindhu became the first Indian to win the Badminton World Championships, she reflected:

"It wasn't about winning a medal; it was about managing myself."

That single line could be the mantra of every Corporate Athlete. It's not about managing deadlines, teams, or deliverables — it's about managing *yourself* at the energy level.

Sindhu structures her training like a rhythm: effort → recovery → reflection → refinement. Each component matters.

Most professionals, however, live in "effort only" mode. They overwork without pause, confusing exhaustion with excellence. The athlete knows better — excellence without recovery collapses into burnout.

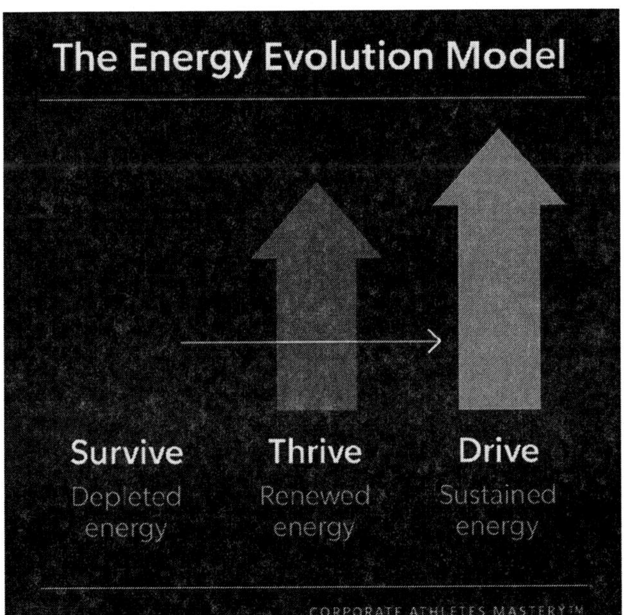

Figure 2 : Energy Evolution Model - From Survival to Sustainable Drive

High performance begins when professionals shift from managing time to managing energy — moving from survival to thriving and ultimately, driving purpose.

Energy — The True Currency of Performance

If time is the stage, energy is the spotlight. Without it, even the best strategy fades in execution.

Every athlete manages energy across **four dimensions**, and so should every professional:

Dimension	Meaning	Neglect Looks Like	Renewal Practice
Physical	The body's stamina and strength	Fatigue, poor sleep, sugar highs	Hydrate, move, stretch, breathe
Emotional	The heart's stability and empathy	Irritability, disengagement	Gratitude, kindness, connection
Mental	The mind's clarity and focus	Distraction, decision fatigue	Deep work, mindfulness, journaling
Spiritual	The soul's alignment with purpose	Meaning drift, burnout	Reflection, values check, purpose reminders

When all four energies align, you experience coherence — a state where your thinking, feeling, and doing are integrated.

Figure 3: Four Dimensions of Energy

The key to corporate stamina isn't working longer — it's working **aligned**.

The 3 PM Dip — A Case of Drained Energy

Arun, a mid-level manager in a tech company, came to coaching with a simple complaint:

"Every afternoon, around 3 p.m., my focus crashes. I can't think straight."

When we explored his day, it became clear: he wasn't tired of work — he was tired of **mismanaged energy**.

- Morning: back-to-back virtual meetings
- Breakfast: just coffee
- Hydration: near zero
- Breaks: none
- Evening: guilt over low output → more hours → poorer sleep

Together, we designed a **micro-recovery plan**:

Time	Energy Ritual
10:30 a.m.	3-minute stretch + 1 glass water
1:00 p.m.	Lunch away from screen
3:00 p.m.	5-minute breathing reset
6:30 p.m.	15-minute reflection walk

Within two weeks, his productivity rose 20%. The number of hours didn't change — the quality of energy did.

This is the **Sindhu mindset in corporate life** — awareness, micro-adjustment, mastery.

Micro-Habits of the Corporate Athlete

Athletes live by rituals, not routines. They design habits that guard energy and focus. Corporate Athletes can do the same by embedding **micro-habits** into daily rhythm.

Here are seven foundational ones:

1. **Begin with breath:** Before opening your inbox, take three slow breaths.
2. **Hydration trigger:** Drink water after every meeting.

3. **90-minute sprints:** Work in deep-focus intervals followed by short breaks.
4. **Move every hour:** Walk during calls; stretch between tasks.
5. **Mindful transition:** Between meetings, pause for 60 seconds.
6. **Evening reflection:** Write one thing you learned and one thing you're grateful for.
7. **Digital sunset:** No screens 30 minutes before sleep.

Each may seem small, but together they reshape your nervous system — from reactive to responsive.

The athlete doesn't seek motivation; they build rhythm. Rhythm sustains motivation naturally.

Emotional Energy — The Missing Muscle

Athletes don't just train their bodies; they train their emotions. The ability to reset quickly after failure determines resilience.

P.V. Sindhu once shared that her coach would make her replay a lost match mentally — not to relive defeat, but to **release** it. The exercise wasn't physical; it was emotional conditioning.

In corporate life, emotional energy leaks through:

- Unspoken frustrations
- Ruminating on feedback
- Comparing yourself to peers
- Holding silent resentment

Emotional mastery isn't suppression; it's **regulation**. It's the ability to name what you feel and choose what you feed.

Try this mini-ritual:

- Notice: "I'm feeling anxious before this call."
- Name: "This is performance pressure."
- Normalize: "It's okay; I've handled this before."
- Navigate: "Let me breathe and focus on what I can control."

That 30-second practice helps you rewire your emotional energy from a reaction to a response.

As Gopichand says, "Winning starts with mastering what happens inside."

Mental Energy — From Focus to Flow

Mental fatigue is the silent killer of creativity. We live in a world of constant cognitive overload — meetings, notifications, decision-making.

Athletes train attention. They enter the "zone" through **focus rituals**: repeating cues, breath control, and visualization.

Corporate athletes can do the same:

- Begin each work block with a **focus anchor** — a simple phrase like *"One task, full presence."*
- Use **digital fasts**: no notifications for one hour daily.
- Practice **mindful attention**: notice distractions without reacting.

Flow isn't luck — it's cultivated clarity. When you align challenge and skill, your brain releases dopamine, endorphins, and serotonin — the "focus cocktail." You feel light yet laser-sharp.

Sindhu describes it perfectly:

"In the best matches, time slows down. I just move, think, and feel in one rhythm."

That rhythm is flow — available to every professional who trains attention like a muscle.

Spiritual Energy — The Power of Purpose

Athletes have a "why" that transcends medals. It anchors them through failure and fatigue.

When Sindhu plays, she represents not just herself but the spirit of possibility for millions. That **purpose** fuels her perseverance.

In corporate life, spiritual energy means working for something larger than the paycheck — impact, service, growth, legacy.

Reflect on these:

- What meaning does my work create?
- Who benefits when I do my best?
- How does this align with my values?

When your **outer game (performance)** aligns with your **inner game (purpose)**, energy renews naturally.

Purpose is not a luxury — it's an energy system. It turns routine tasks into meaningful contributions.

The Energy Audit — Awareness Practice

Take 10 quiet minutes. Draw four quadrants labeled **Physical, Emotional, Mental, and Spiritual**.

Ask yourself:

1. How full is my energy in each area (1–10)?
2. Where am I leaking energy?
3. What one habit could recharge that area this week?

Example:

- Physical = 6 → start 15-min morning walk
- Emotional = 5 → express gratitude daily
- Mental = 7 → reduce multitasking
- Spiritual = 4 → reconnect with purpose

Energy awareness is the first step to energy mastery.

Coaching Insight — The Energy Mirror

Leaders who coach understand that performance conversations are also **energy conversations**. When an employee struggles, instead of asking *"Why are you not performing?"*, ask:

"Where do you feel drained — physically, emotionally, mentally, or spiritually?"

This shift changes judgment into partnership. It allows people to take ownership of their energy patterns.

As one CEO client once said after introducing this reflection practice:

"We stopped managing performance and started managing presence — and everything changed."

Renewal Rituals — Designing Your Rhythm

Create a personal energy blueprint:

Moment	Purpose	Practice
Morning	Activation	Gratitude, visualization, hydration
Midday	Regulation	Breath break, quick walk
Afternoon	Recovery	Stretch, laughter, short reflection
Evening	Reflection	Journaling, digital sunset, sleep ritual

Your goal isn't balance — it's rhythm. Balance is static; rhythm is alive.

Athletes don't seek balance. They **oscillate** between training and rest, focus and flow, silence and sprint. That's the sustainable model for modern professionals.

The Survive → Thrive → Drive Model

Every professional moves through three stages of energy evolution:

Stage	Description	Focus Shift
Survive	Doing more with less: energy depletion	From coping to caring for energy

Thrive	Sustainable rhythm; renewed motivation	From effort to awareness
Drive	Peak purpose, flow, and mastery	From success to significance

Athletes train to move beyond survival mode into flow. Corporate athletes do the same by redesigning days around energy rhythm, not time pressure.

Case Story — Leena's Recharge Habit

Leena, a marketing head, began noticing her patience thinning. Small irritations triggered outsized reactions. She realized it wasn't attitude — it was **energy debt**.

Through coaching, she introduced a "pause protocol":

- 5 minutes between meetings for breathwork.
- 1 screen-free meal daily.
- 1 "white space" hour weekly for creative thought.

Six months later, her team described her as "calmer, clearer, and more inspiring." Her output didn't increase dramatically — but her **impact multiplied**.

That's the paradox of energy: When you slow down deliberately, your results accelerate.

Reflection — Designing Your Energy Legacy

Take a deep breath. Reflect:

- What drains me most during my week?
- What recharges me deeply?
- How do I show up when my energy is full?
- What rituals would my best self keep sacred?

Write them down. The page becomes your first **training plan** as a Corporate Athlete.

Closing Reflection

You began your career as an employee managing tasks. Now, you evolve into an athlete managing energy — your most renewable, powerful, and personal resource.

Energy mastery transforms busyness into brilliance. It's how champions like Sindhu sustain excellence year after year — not by doing more, but by doing what matters **with full presence**.

When you master energy, you stop running out of time — because every moment becomes fully lived.

KEY TAKEAWAYS

☑ Time is finite; energy is renewable.
☑ Performance depends on managing four energies — physical, emotional, mental, and spiritual.
☑ Micro-habits create macro results.
☑ Awareness is the first step to mastery.
☑ Energy alignment enables sustained excellence.

"You don't need more time; you need more energy, focus, and purpose — the true fuel of a Corporate Athlete."

Coach Yourself: Reflection Exercises

1. Rate yourself on each energy dimension (1–10).
2. Which one drains most quickly — and why?
3. What micro-habit can you add to renew it this week?
4. When are you at your best energy — and how can you design more of those moments?
5. What would your rhythm of sustainable performance look like?

Chapter 3

THE PLAYER — PERFORMING WITH EXCELLENCE

Mastering Discipline, Focus, and the Joy of Continuous Growth

---

"Before you can lead or coach others, you must first master your own game."

– Kishore Kumar Thakur, Corporate Athletes!

The Arena of the Player

Every athlete begins as a **player** — someone who steps into the arena not to prove others wrong, but to prove themselves right.

In that first moment — the whistle blows, the crowd fades, and all that remains is the rhythm of breath, heartbeat, and will.

In corporate life, you enter a similar arena every day — your office, your first meeting, your next presentation, your next decision. The stakes may not be measured in medals, but the pressure feels no less real.

As a Player, you are tested constantly — not by opponents, but by distractions. Not by the crowd, but by the quiet voice in your head that asks, *"Am I good enough?"*

To perform with excellence, you must do what all champions do — train not just your skills, but your **state**. Because mastery begins the day you stop chasing perfection and start practicing presence.

"Champions are not made in the arena; they are revealed there."

The Player's journey is one of devotion — showing up every day with focus, humility, and hunger.

The Discipline of Greatness: Virat Kohli's Transformation

When Virat Kohli burst onto the cricket scene in 2008, he was talented but raw — known for aggression, passion, and flashes of brilliance. But talent alone does not sustain greatness.

In 2012, after a poor tour of Australia, Kohli had a realization: he wasn't yet the athlete he wanted to be. He was performing on skill but not sustaining it through the system. That was the moment of his metamorphosis — the transformation from **player of potential** to **player of discipline**.

He changed everything. His diet, his sleep, his training, his mindset — everything revolved around one central question:

"How can I become the fittest version of myself — not just the best batsman?"

That decision changed not only his career but the culture of Indian cricket. Kohli became the standard-bearer of **professionalism, fitness, and mental focus**.

He turned practice into a ritual. He trained even on off days. He visualized success not through luck but through preparation.

His morning routine became sacred. Early wake-up. Strength and conditioning. Fielding drills. Visualization.

He once said:

"I hate losing more than I love winning. But I've learned that preparation is the only antidote to fear."

Kohli's career became a masterclass in the **discipline of excellence**. He didn't just raise his batting average — he raised the bar for what it means to be a professional.

He embodied what every Corporate Athlete must learn: **Talent opens the door. Discipline keeps it open.**

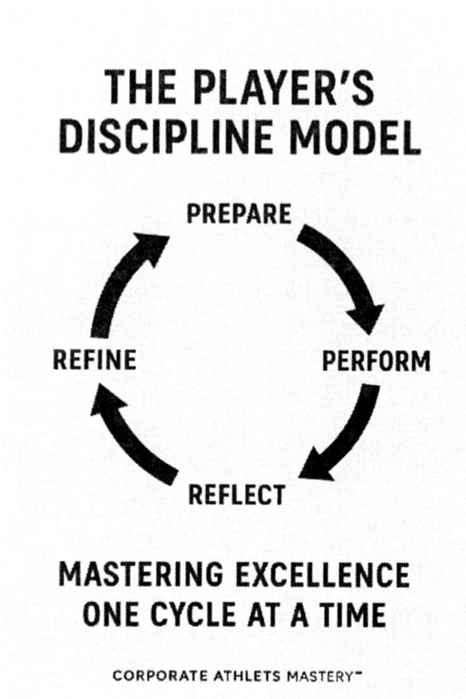

Figure 4: The Players Discipline Model

"The greats don't practice until they get it right. They practice until they can't get it wrong."

Discipline in the Corporate Arena

In the corporate world, discipline doesn't mean rigidity — it means reliability. It means showing up consistently, even when no one is watching. It means doing the small things well — day after day — because you respect your craft.

Imagine if every presentation, client call, or project review was treated like a match that mattered — not because of who's watching, but because it's an opportunity to play your best game.

That's the Player's mindset: **every performance counts**. Not for perfection, but for progress.

Story of Reinvention: Mary Kom — The Relentless Fighter

If discipline defines consistency, reinvention defines longevity.

Mary Kom's story is one of the most powerful examples of **sustained excellence through renewal**.

Nicknamed *Magnificent Mary*, she is a six-time world champion and an Olympic medalist — but her greatness lies beyond her medals.

After becoming a mother of twins, many believed her boxing career was over. But Mary Kom refused to accept that her best days were behind her. With fierce determination, she trained harder than ever — balancing motherhood, family, and sport with grace and grit.

When asked how she managed it all, she said:

"The ring doesn't know if you're a mother or a rookie. It only knows how prepared you are."

That line should be framed in every workplace. The boardroom, like the boxing ring, doesn't care about your titles, background, or story — it responds to your **preparation and mindset**.

Mary Kom's comeback wasn't just physical — it was emotional and spiritual. She fought not against opponents, but against assumptions — society's and her own. She turned every doubt into data. Every loss into a learning.

That's the essence of the Player mindset — you evolve not by avoiding failure but by transforming it into feedback.

Practice Over Perfection

Athletes spend 90% of their time practicing and 10% performing. Corporate professionals often do the reverse — performing all day, every day, with little time to deliberately improve.

When you stop practicing, you start plateauing. Practice is the laboratory where excellence is refined.

For the Corporate Athlete, practice doesn't just mean rehearsing presentations. It means:

- Reviewing performance honestly.
- Seeking feedback without defensiveness.
- Reflecting on what worked and what didn't.

A leader once told me, "I attend 40 meetings a week, but I never review a single one." That's like a cricketer who plays every match but never analyzes their batting.

Excellence demands **reflection time** — what athletes call *"film study."*

"You can't improve what you don't review."

So, before your next big meeting or project, pause and ask:

- What's my goal?
- What mindset do I need to bring?
- How will I measure success?

And after it's done, ask again:

- What worked well?
- What could I do better next time?

This small ritual turns experience into expertise.

The Science of Focus and Flow

Performance is not just about effort; it's about **state**. Athletes call it being *in the zone*. Neuroscientists call it *flow*.

In flow, your brain releases dopamine, endorphins, and norepinephrine — chemicals that heighten concentration and lower self-doubt. Time slows. Execution feels effortless.

Kohli often describes this state:

"When I bat at my best, I don't think. The ball just comes. I react. It's like I disappear into the game."

Flow happens when **challenge and skill are balanced**. Too much challenge causes anxiety. Too little causes boredom.

To enter flow, professionals must design focus rituals — cues that signal the brain it's time to perform. For example:

- Taking three deep breaths before a meeting.
- Listening to a specific instrumental track before a pitch.
- Visualizing success, not as pressure, but as rhythm.

The brain loves patterns. When you create rituals, you reduce cognitive load and increase clarity. That's how you perform with grace under pressure.

The Inner Game of the Player

Performance is as much about what happens inside as outside.

Every athlete fights two battles — one with the opponent and one within. The inner battle is against fear, doubt, ego, and fatigue.

In corporate life, the inner game is about managing these internal triggers:

- The fear of failure.
- The temptation of multitasking.
- The craving for validation.
- The fatigue of constant proving.

Kohli once admitted that early in his career, he cared too much about what others thought. He was fuelled by criticism, but also drained by it. Over time, he learned to replace validation with **self-trust**.

That's the essence of mastery — shifting from external approval to internal alignment.

Mary Kom echoed the same when she said:

"When I fight for a purpose, I'm unstoppable. When I fight for approval, I'm uncertain."

As a Corporate Athlete, your best performance comes not when you chase recognition but when you serve your mission.

Case Story: Ravi's Pre-Performance Ritual

Ravi, a senior sales manager, once confessed:

"Every presentation feels like a performance — I get anxious and overthink."

Together, we built his "Player's Ritual":

Step 1 — Prepare the State, Not the Slides: He stopped rehearsing only content and started preparing his mindset — breathing, stretching, and visualizing.

Step 2 — Rehearse Recovery: Between presentations, he did a two-minute reset — slow exhalation and posture correction.

Step 3 — Review Immediately: After each session, he jotted down what worked and what didn't while it was still fresh.

Within three months, his confidence soared. Clients described him as "calm, centered, and magnetic."

Ravi hadn't changed his skills — he had mastered his **state**.

That's what being a Player is about — performing with energy, focus, and flow, regardless of external chaos.

The Three Anchors of Consistency

Every elite performer builds their consistency on three invisible anchors:

Anchor	Meaning	Daily Practice
Preparation	Respecting the process	Plan, rehearse, visualize
Presence	Being fully engaged	One task, full attention
Purpose	Knowing your "why"	Connect effort with meaning

Without preparation, performance collapses under pressure. Without presence, talent disperses into distraction. Without purpose, work turns mechanical.

Together, these three create the **architecture of excellence**.

The Reflection Locker Room

Every athlete needs a locker room — a space to reset, recover, and reflect. In corporate life, that space must be created deliberately.

Try this 10-minute reflection exercise at the end of your day:

1. **Play of the Day:** What moment today made me feel proud or fulfilled?

2. **Learning of the Day:** What did I discover about myself or my work?
3. **Let Go:** What can I release before tomorrow?
   Reflection turns your day from activity into awareness. It's where performance becomes wisdom.

The Invisible Practice of Character

Athletes train muscles. Corporate Athletes train **character**.

Character is how you behave when things don't go your way — when the deal falls through, the promotion doesn't come, the effort isn't noticed.

Mary Kom once lost a world championship bout due to a controversial decision. When reporters asked if she was angry, she smiled and said:

"The judges can take my points, not my purpose."

That's mastery — refusing to let external unfairness define internal peace.

In every organization, people watch how you respond under pressure. That's when leadership begins — long before the title arrives.

As you grow as a Player, remember: **Character outlasts skill. Mindset outperforms mechanics.**

The Survive–Thrive–Drive Lens

In Chapter 2, we explored how individuals evolve from surviving to thriving to driving. At the Player level, these stages look like this:

Phase	Energy Focus	Behavioral Shift
Survive	Coping with tasks	Reacts to pressure
Thrive	Managing state	Responds with awareness
Drive	Performing with purpose	Inspires others through example

Athletes live in "drive" because they train awareness. Professionals often stay in "survive" because they ignore recovery.

To shift from survive to drive, treat every day like a micro-tournament — plan, perform, recover, reflect, repeat.

Reflection Practice — Your Player's Journal

Take a notebook — your personal **Performance Journal** — and answer weekly:

1. What did I prepare well for this week?
2. When was I most focused and alive?
3. Where did I lose energy or discipline?
4. What's one thing I'll refine next week?

These reflections build self-trust — the foundation of excellence.

The Player's Creed

I am the player of my own game.
My discipline is my strength.
My focus is my weapon.
My practice is my preparation.
I play not to prove, but to improve.
I perform not to please, but to progress.
I am not driven by perfection, but by purpose.
Every day, I rise — not to win, but to evolve.

This creed is the mindset of every Corporate Athlete who performs not out of fear, but out of faith — in their craft, their process, and their presence.

Closing Reflection

Being a Player is about one thing: **ownership**. Owning your energy, your preparation, your performance, your growth.

When you take ownership, you stop waiting for perfect conditions. You realize that *discipline is freedom*, and *practice is power.*

Virat Kohli built consistency through discipline. Mary Kom built longevity through reinvention. You can build both through awareness.

The Player within you is not waiting for applause — only for alignment. Play your game with focus, rhythm, and grace. Because every meeting is a match. Every day is a training ground. And your career — it's your championship.

KEY TAKEAWAYS

☑ Performance is a practice, not an event.
☑ Discipline creates consistency; reinvention sustains longevity.
☑ Reflection turns experience into mastery.
☑ Flow happens when challenge and skill align.
☑ Character and awareness define true performance.

"Excellence is not doing extraordinary things once — it's doing ordinary things extraordinarily well, every single day."

Coach Yourself: Reflection Exercises

1. What daily rituals prepare you for high performance?
2. When are you most "in the zone" — and what triggers it?
3. How do you recover and reflect after intense days?
4. Where do you see discipline as restriction instead of freedom?
5. What would it mean for you to "play your game" with purpose?

Chapter 4

THE CAPTAIN – LEADING WITH VISION AND COURAGE

Balancing Results, Relationships, and Responsibility

"The mark of a great leader is not how loudly they command, but how clearly they inspire."

From Player to Captain: The Shift from Performance to Presence

When you begin your journey as a professional, your primary focus is on **individual excellence** — hitting your targets, mastering your craft, and being recognized for your skill. That's the **Player stage** — where discipline and consistency define your success.

But eventually, your work begins to expand beyond you. People start looking up to you for guidance, not just output. Your results now depend not only on your effort, but on the collective energy, trust, and alignment of those around you.

That's when you step into the next arena — the **Captain stage**.

Being a Captain is not about hierarchy or authority. It's about *influence, clarity, and courage.* It's about holding vision steady in the middle of uncertainty — when others feel lost, tired, or afraid.

A Player wins the match. A Captain builds a team that can win without them.

That's leadership maturity — when your purpose expands from *winning for yourself* to *creating the conditions for others to win.*

The Leadership Paradox

In the modern workplace, leaders are constantly balancing paradoxes:

- **Strong yet empathetic.**
- **Decisive yet inclusive.**
- **Ambitious yet patient.**
- **Strategic yet grounded.**

To lead in today's environment, you must learn to hold these opposites together — with awareness and balance.

Leadership is no longer about control. It's about **creating clarity, enabling trust, and amplifying strengths.**

This is not easy — because leadership magnifies pressure. You are no longer judged by your own output, but by the culture you create. The higher you rise, the less feedback you receive — and the more you need self-awareness to stay grounded.

And that's where the true essence of The Captain emerges: **Leading with calm, courage, and clarity — even in chaos.**

Story: M.S. Dhoni — Calmness in the Chaos

Few leaders embody that essence better than **Mahendra Singh Dhoni**, one of India's most iconic captains — not only in cricket, but in the art of leadership itself.

Dhoni's story is not just about victories — it's about *vision, trust, and composure under fire*. It's about leading with **stillness**, not noise.

The Early Lessons of Leadership

When Dhoni first took charge of Team India in 2007, he wasn't the most senior player. In fact, many in the team had far more experience. But he had something extraordinary — *emotional intelligence and the ability to make people believe in themselves.*

During the inaugural T20 World Cup, India's young squad was full of raw talent but lacked international exposure. The world expected them to falter.

Dhoni, however, led with simplicity. He encouraged each player to express themselves, to trust their instincts, to play without fear. And when the pressure mounted — in the semifinal against Australia and the final against Pakistan — his composure became the team's anchor.

Even in moments when the match swung wildly, he stood behind the stumps — quiet, observant, smiling. No shouting. No panic. Just presence.

Leadership in Stillness

In one post-match interview, a journalist asked Dhoni:

"How do you stay so calm under pressure?"

He replied with characteristic humility:

"If I panic, my team panics. So I choose to stay calm."

That single sentence captures the essence of **The Captain's Mindset** — leadership not as performance, but as presence.

In high-stress environments — whether in a cricket field or a corporate boardroom — emotions are contagious. A leader's energy sets the emotional tone for the team. When you stay centered, others find their center through you.

That's why Dhoni's calm was not passive — it was **strategic composure**. He understood that leadership is not about being the loudest voice in the room; it's about being the most grounded.

Trusting the Team

Dhoni's greatness also lay in his ability to **trust his players completely**.

In the 2011 World Cup final, he made one of the most discussed decisions in Indian cricket history — promoting himself up the batting order ahead of the in-form Yuvraj Singh.

Many were surprised. It was a bold, risky call. But Dhoni knew the conditions, the bowlers, and most importantly, the psychological rhythm of his team. He didn't take that decision to be a hero. He took it to stabilize the innings and take responsibility.

He walked in with quiet determination — and when he finished the match with a six over long-on, it wasn't just a victory for India. It was a **masterclass in accountability**.

That six wasn't an act of glory — it was an act of ownership.

Translating Dhoni's Lessons to Corporate Leadership

Every corporate leader faces Dhoni moments — situations where the team looks uncertain, where stakes are high, and clarity is fogged by pressure.

Dhoni teaches us that leadership doesn't mean knowing everything. It means **creating an environment where others can give their best.**

Here's what The Captain's mindset looks like in the workplace:

Dhoni's Leadership Trait	Corporate Application
Calm under pressure	Respond to crises with clarity, not chaos
Trusting others	Empower teams to own their results
Taking responsibility	Step forward in critical moments
Leading by example	Show consistency, not control
Prioritizing the team	Put collective goals above ego

In one organization I coached, a senior project director, *Rajesh*, faced a massive delivery challenge. Tight deadlines, technical issues, and a stressed-out team. Everyone looked to him for direction.

Instead of diving into micromanagement, he said calmly:

"We'll get through this if we stay patient. Let's fix one problem at a time."

His composure became contagious. The team stopped panicking, started prioritizing, and delivered on time.

Afterward, one team member said,

"We didn't need more instructions — we needed his calm."

That's the Dhoni effect — the power of **presence-led leadership**.

From Control to Trust

Early in your leadership journey, it's natural to rely on control — checking, monitoring, and approving every detail. But that's like trying to play every ball yourself.

The evolution from Player to Captain begins the day you realize that your job is no longer to *do everything right*, but to *make others believe they can.*

Trust is not naïve optimism. It's a deliberate act of empowerment.

When you trust people, you transfer ownership. When you transfer ownership, you unleash commitment.

As a Captain, your greatest strength lies not in giving answers — but in asking questions that awaken others' confidence.

The Captain's Stillness: A Mirror for Modern Leadership

In today's corporate arena — where change is relentless and uncertainty is constant — leaders who stay grounded become organizational anchors.

When you stay calm:

- Your team mirrors your energy.
- Your decisions become clearer.
- Your influence grows silently but powerfully.

This doesn't mean suppressing emotion. It means mastering your energy — so you can manage the energy of the team.

Dhoni once said:

"You don't control results, but you can control your reactions."

That line could be the mantra of every modern leader.

Reflection: The Calm Within the Storm

Take a moment to pause and reflect:

1. How do you typically respond when pressure rises — with clarity or with urgency?
2. What does "calmness under chaos" mean to you in your professional context?
3. When was the last time your composure inspired others?

4. What would change if your calm became your team's confidence?

These reflections mark the transition from **performer** to **leader** — from *The Player* who executes to *The Captain* who elevates.

Dhoni's leadership teaches us about *emotional stability and trust.* But leadership also demands **courage in adversity** — the ability to inspire belief when everything seems to be falling apart.

For that, we turn to another extraordinary leader — **Rani Rampal**, the captain of India's women's hockey team.

Her story is not just about winning tournaments — it's about *breaking barriers*, *building belonging*, and *leading with heart.*

Story: Rani Rampal – The Power of Purposeful Leadership

In the world of Indian sports, few stories capture resilience and leadership transformation like **Rani Rampal's** — the captain who led India's women's hockey team to the Olympic semifinals after decades.

Her story is not about privilege. It's about perseverance.

From Barefoot to the World Stage

Rani was born in a small town near Karnal, Haryana, into a modest family. Her father drove a horse cart. Her home often flooded during the rains. She played hockey with a broken stick because they couldn't afford a real one.

When she was 14, she made it to the national team. But what defined her wasn't talent alone — it was hunger.

In one interview, she said:

"I didn't want to play hockey just to wear the India jersey. I wanted to change what people thought was possible for girls like me."

That sentence captures the essence of **The Captain's Purpose** — leadership that transcends personal ambition and touches collective transformation.

Turning Pain into Power

When Rani became captain in 2017, the team had talent but lacked belief. Years of underfunding, limited exposure, and societal barriers had taken their toll.

She didn't begin with strategies or speeches. She began with **connection** — listening to her teammates' stories, understanding their fears, and building trust.

She created a simple ritual before every match: Each player would share what they were playing for — their "why."

Some played for their families, some for pride, some for freedom. Rani listened and said,

"Then let's play not just for medals, but for every girl who dreams like we did."

That was her vision — to make hockey a symbol of possibility.

Leadership Under Fire

The 2021 Tokyo Olympics became a defining moment. After two heartbreaking early losses, the team could have collapsed under pressure. But Rani held them together with quiet conviction.

She said to her teammates:

"We've already proved we belong here. Now let's show the world how much we've grown."

That one line reframed defeat into opportunity. It turned anxiety into courage.

India went on to beat Australia in the quarterfinals — one of the biggest upsets in Olympic history — and finished fourth overall. Though they missed a medal, they won something greater — **belief**.

What Rani Teaches Us About Leadership

Rani's leadership wasn't about commanding excellence — it was about **awakening belief**. She transformed her team not through fear, but through **shared purpose and trust**.

Her style reveals three powerful lessons for every corporate leader:

Leadership Quality	Rani Rampal's Practice	Corporate Reflection
Purpose	Defined a "why" beyond results	Connect team goals to a meaningful purpose

Empathy	Understood every player's story	Lead with listening before directing
Courage	Faced global giants with calm conviction	Stand steady in uncertainty and inspire hope

This is leadership that flows not from authority, but **authenticity**. Rani's journey reminds us that courage is not the absence of fear — it's the presence of purpose stronger than fear.

The Leadership Paradox: Balancing Head and Heart

In modern organizations, leaders face a paradox similar to what athletes experience on the field: They must deliver results under pressure — yet sustain morale under uncertainty.

They must be ambitious enough to push forward, yet grounded enough to pause and reflect.

That's the **Leadership Paradox**: Balancing head and heart, results and relationships, performance and presence.

Most leaders tilt too far one way — either becoming too results-driven (risking burnout and disengagement) or too relationship-driven (risking complacency).

The art of the Captain lies in finding the **dynamic balance between the two** — the ability to move fluidly between driving and listening, challenging and supporting.

Rani Rampal did that instinctively. She demanded excellence but offered empathy. She pushed hard but held space for emotion. She embodied **grace under pressure**.

And that's what every modern Captain must cultivate — the ability to **stay centered amidst contradiction**.

- **The Captain's Compass: Vision Connection Courage**

Every great leader navigates with an inner compass — a set of guiding forces that keep them steady, even when the environment shifts.

The **Captain's Compass** consists of three forces that define conscious leadership:

Vision – Seeing Beyond the Immediate

Connection – Building Trust and Belonging

Courage – Standing Tall in Uncertainty

Together, they form the **Leadership Triangle** — balancing direction, empathy, and conviction.

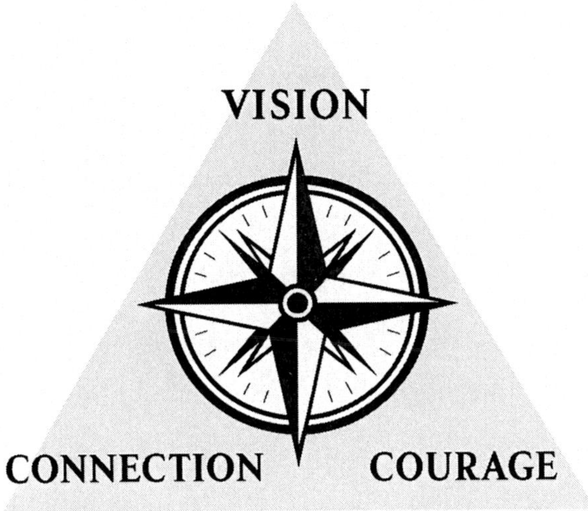

The Captain's Leadership Triangle

Figure 5: The Captain's Compass — Vision Connection Courage

- *Balanced leaders navigate through clarity of purpose, depth of empathy, and strength of conviction.*

Vision: The North Star

Vision is the ability to see beyond the visible — to imagine what could be, even before the evidence appears.

For Captains, vision is not a statement on a wall; it's a feeling in people's hearts. It's what turns goals into meaning.

When you share a vision clearly, you ignite intrinsic motivation. Your team stops working for you — they start working with you.

Corporate Reflection:

"Before every project or meeting, remind your team: *Why does this matter — to the customer, the company, and to us?*"

Vision is not just direction — it's a connection to purpose.

Connection: The Heart of Leadership

Connection is the bridge between people and purpose. It's built not in speeches but in small, consistent acts of care.

True connection is created when people feel seen, heard, and valued. In a coaching session with a technology firm's senior manager, she said,

"My team doesn't need me to motivate them — they need me to believe in them."

That's connection — the invisible thread that strengthens trust.

In sports, we see this when a captain pats a bowler after a bad over, or when a leader huddles the team after a loss. Those small gestures rebuild energy faster than any strategy.

Connection is emotional currency — and trust is its compound interest.

Story: Dhoni and the Trophy That Defined Leadership

When India won the 2011 ICC Cricket World Cup, millions waited for Captain M.S. Dhoni to lift the trophy first. He was the strategist, the finisher, the calm center of the storm. But when that moment came, Dhoni quietly stepped back and let his teammates — especially the younger players and senior legends — take the stage.

He stood behind them, smiling. No grand gestures, no speeches. Just presence.

That quiet act spoke louder than any celebration. It said, *"This victory belongs to all of us."*

True leadership isn't about being the hero in the spotlight — it's about creating space for others to rise. Dhoni showed what connection really means: trust, humility, and the courage to share success.

Great Captains don't just lead teams to victory; they teach their teams to believe they can win without them.

Courage: The Backbone of Leadership

Courage is not dramatic. It's deeply personal. It's the decision to do what's right, even when it's hard.

In corporate life, courage shows up when you:

- Admit a mistake publicly.
- Ask for feedback from your team.
- Say "no" to unethical shortcuts.
- Defend your people in tough times.

Courage doesn't mean absence of fear. It means the presence of clarity.

Rani Rampal once said after the Olympics:

"We may not have a medal, but we have respect — and that's harder to earn."

That's courage — redefining success on your own terms.

The Captain's Compass in Action

When you integrate Vision, Connection, and Courage, you move from managing to inspiring.

Force	Outcome When Practiced
Vision	Creates clarity and motivation
Connection	Builds trust and loyalty
Courage	Inspires respect and authenticity

Without **Vision**, teams lose direction. Without **Connection**, they lose cohesion. Without **Courage**, they lose conviction.

Leadership maturity means knowing when to lean into each — and how to use all three in harmony.

Mini Practice: The Captain's Daily Check-In

Before you end your day, ask yourself:

- **Vision:** Did I remind my team why their work matters?
- **Connection:** Did I listen more than I spoke today?
- **Courage:** Did I take one difficult action aligned with my values?

If you can answer "yes" to even two, you're growing as a Captain.

Reflection: Your Leadership Compass

1. What is the vision that currently guides your work?
2. How do you create a connection with your team, beyond meetings and metrics?
3. Where do you need to act with greater courage right now?
4. What would it look like if you led with all three forces in balance?

Leadership begins the moment you start asking deeper questions of yourself — not just your team.

We have now seen leadership through the eyes of Dhoni — composure under pressure — and Rani Rampal — courage in adversity. Both show us that leadership is not a performance, but a practice.

Yet there is another dimension of Captaincy — **wisdom and humility**. The ability to lead with quiet strength, to develop others, and to step back gracefully when the time comes.

That brings us to the next part of our journey — the leadership philosophy of **Rahul Dravid**, known affectionately as *The Wall* — a captain whose legacy is built not on volume, but on values.

Story: Rahul Dravid – The Grace of Servant Leadership

If M.S. Dhoni symbolizes calm courage and Rani Rampal embodies inspiring belief, then **Rahul Dravid** represents something quieter — *integrity, patience, and service-minded leadership.*

His leadership style wasn't flashy. He didn't raise his voice, seek headlines, or chase credit. Yet his influence shaped generations.

He taught us that leadership isn't about being the hero — it's about *building others into heroes.*

Leadership Through Example

In the early 2000s, Rahul Dravid was already one of India's most dependable batsmen. But what stood out wasn't his talent — it was his temperament. He was the player who anchored the innings when wickets fell, the one who absorbed pressure without losing grace.

When he became captain, India was in a period of transition. There were expectations, egos, and enormous scrutiny.

Yet Dravid led not with charisma, but with **character**. He modeled professionalism so consistently that his presence itself became a standard.

In one post-match conference, a journalist asked him about his leadership philosophy. He said simply:

"Leadership is about making people around you better — even when it costs you comfort."

That one sentence captures the spirit of servant leadership — leadership that prioritizes the growth of others above self-glory.

The Dravid Way: Still Water Runs Deep

One of the most iconic moments of his leadership came in 2007 during a test match in South Africa. A young fast bowler, **S. Sreesanth**, had taken a wicket and celebrated exuberantly in front of the batter, nearly provoking a confrontation.

The cameras caught Dravid calling him over quietly. He didn't scold him. He put a hand on his shoulder, whispered something brief — and Sreesanth simply nodded and smiled.

Later, when asked what Dravid had said, Sreesanth replied:

"He just said — 'Well bowled. Next time, let your performance do the talking.'"

That is leadership through dignity. He did not correct behavior through fear, but through **example and empathy**. And it worked — because respect given freely is respect returned deeply.

Leadership as Service

After his international career, Rahul Dravid didn't seek commentary or limelight. He chose to head the **National Cricket Academy (NCA)** and later coached India's under-19 and "A" teams.

It was a quiet decision — but one that shaped India's future. Under his guidance, young players like Shubman Gill,

Rishabh Pant, and Prithvi Shaw learned not just technique, but temperament.

Dravid's coaching philosophy is simple:

"My job is not to create the next Dravid — it's to create the next better version of each player."

That line embodies the heart of The Captain's evolution — moving from *leading for success* to *leading for succession.*

Leadership, at its peak, is about **legacy through others**.

The Corporate Parallel

In corporate environments, leaders often rise because of their performance — but they remain relevant because of their ability to **grow others**.

One senior executive I coached, *Anita*, shared something remarkable. After being promoted to director, she realized that her success now depended less on her own output and more on the growth of her managers. She said,

"I used to measure my worth by what I achieved. Now, I measure it by how many people I've helped advance."

That's the Dravid mindset — leadership not as spotlight, but as stewardship.

The most powerful Captains eventually become Coaches. They realize that the purpose of leadership is not control, but **continuity**.

The Captain's Inner Game: Mastery of Ego

Every Captain battles one invisible opponent — the **ego**. It whispers, *"You're the reason for success. You're the leader because you know best."*

But ego narrows vision and disconnects leaders from their teams.

The greatest leaders know when to step back. When to let others shine. When to say, *"It's your moment now."*

Rahul Dravid did that when he handed over captaincy to M.S. Dhoni, supporting the younger leader wholeheartedly. He didn't cling to control — he enabled continuity.

That moment showed that humility is not weakness — it's wisdom. The ability to serve when you could dominate, and to guide when you could command.

In the words of Nelson Mandela:

"A leader is like a shepherd. He stays behind the flock, letting the most nimble go ahead, whereupon the others follow — not realizing all along that he is directing them from behind."

That's the Dravid way — leading quietly, guiding deeply.

The Captain's Oath

At this stage of your Corporate Athlete journey, The Captain's Oath becomes your compass — a daily reminder of what true leadership stands for.

You may choose to print this, frame it, or reflect on it during your leadership rituals.

The Captain's Oath

I lead not to control, but to cultivate.
I speak not to impress, but to inspire.
I decide not to dominate, but to empower.
I hold a vision when others doubt.
I build trust when others retreat.
I act with courage when fear prevails.
I balance results with relationships, ambition with awareness, power with purpose.
I lead from clarity, not certainty — from calm, not chaos.
I remember that leadership is not about me, but about what I awaken in others.

This oath represents the *inner evolution of the Captain* — from a performer who leads tasks to a transformer who leads hearts.

Reflection: The Captain's Mirror

Take a quiet moment to pause and reflect on your own leadership journey.

Ask yourself:

1. What kind of energy do people feel when they leave a meeting with me?

2. Do I lead with clarity — or just with urgency?
3. When was the last time I took a decision that reflected courage, not comfort?
4. Who in my team needs belief more than direction?
5. What would change if I measured leadership not by performance, but by presence?

Leadership awareness begins not in grand decisions, but in small daily choices.

Closing Reflections — The Captain's Legacy

Leadership is not about being in charge. It's about taking charge *of yourself first*, so you can serve others better.

The Captain's journey is the bridge between **self-mastery (Player)** and **selfless mastery (Coach)**. It's where excellence transforms into influence — and influence into impact.

Every Captain learns that leadership doesn't end when the match does — it continues in how you lift others after the game.

When M.S. Dhoni handed the trophy to his teammates first, when Rani Rampal hugged her players after a loss, when Rahul Dravid stayed in the shadows of his students' success — they all showed us one truth:

Leadership is not about being followed. It's about leaving behind people who no longer need to be led.

As The Captain evolves, a new dimension of leadership begins to unfold — **The Coach.**

Where the Captain leads through vision and courage, the Coach leads through awareness and empathy.

In the next chapter, we will explore what it means to grow others — not by instructing, but by *illuminating*. You'll discover how coaching is not a role — but a mindset that transforms both people and culture.

KEY TAKEAWAYS

- ☑ Leadership maturity is the ability to balance Vision, Connection, and Courage.
- ☑ Calmness and clarity are stronger than control.
- ☑ True leaders grow others — they don't guard authority.
- ☑ Humility is the ultimate mark of confidence.
- ☑ The Captain's journey ends not with applause, but with legacy.

"A true leader is not the loudest voice in the room, but the calmest heart in the storm."

Chapter 5

THE COACH – GROWING OTHERS AND SELF

Cultivating Awareness, Empathy, and Empowerment

"A great coach doesn't give answers — they create the space for answers to emerge."

From Leader to Coach – The Shift of Mindset

When you reach the Captain stage of your professional journey, you've learned to perform and to lead. You've mastered focus, you've inspired teams, and you've balanced strategy and empathy. But at some point, a deeper calling emerges — a shift from **driving results** to **developing people**.

That is the birth of *The Coach.*

The Player mastered the skill. The Captain mastered influence. The Coach masters *awareness and growth — in self and others.*

A Coach's success is not measured by how much they accomplish, but by how much they help others discover within themselves.

From Instruction to Inquiry

Traditional leadership often begins with instruction — telling, directing, guiding. But coaching begins with *inquiry* — asking, listening, reflecting.

The Coach does not say, "Here's what you should do." They ask, "What do you think will make this work?"

It's a subtle, yet profound shift. Because questions awaken ownership, while answers breed dependence.

The Gopichand Way – The Architect of Excellence

Few stories illustrate this transformation better than **Pullela Gopichand**, the man who turned India into a badminton powerhouse.

After a brilliant playing career — including the 2001 All England title — Gopichand could have chosen comfort, commentary, or celebrity. Instead, he chose contribution.

He sold his own land, invested his savings, and built the **Gopichand Badminton Academy** in Hyderabad — a place that would nurture champions like Saina Nehwal, P.V. Sindhu, and Kidambi Srikanth.

When asked *why* he did it, his answer was simple:

"If I can help one more athlete dream bigger, play better, and live stronger — it's worth everything."

That's the heart of coaching — legacy through others.

The Discipline Behind Empathy

Gopichand is often described as calm and composed. But behind that serenity lies uncompromising discipline. His academy begins training at 4 a.m. He believes in consistency more than charisma.

One of his protégés recalls:

"He never scolded us. He simply asked, 'Did you give your 100% today?' That question haunted you — because it made you reflect."

A true coach doesn't pressure — they provoke *awareness*. They help you see what you don't yet see.

Coaching as Service

When players falter, Gopichand doesn't ask, "What went wrong?" He asks, "What did you learn?"

That single change in language transforms failure from fear into feedback.

In organizations, too, coaching leadership reframes mistakes as learning loops. Instead of, "Why did this fail?" try asking, "What insight can we carry forward?"

Coaches turn judgment into growth.

Corporate Parallel

In a leadership workshop for a tech firm, a senior manager once told me:

"I've spent years fixing people's problems. Now I realize my real job is to help them think for themselves."

That's the moment a manager becomes a Coach.

Because fixing is faster — but developing is deeper. Coaching is the art of *slowing down to speed up performance.*

The Coaching Mindset – Three Core Pillars

Through decades of sports and executive coaching, three qualities consistently appear in the best coaches — **Curiosity, Empathy, and Empowerment.**

These are not techniques; they're *ways of being.*

Pillar	Mindset Shift	In Practice
Curiosity	From knowing to exploring	Ask open questions that invite insight
Empathy	From judging to understanding	Listen beyond words – to feelings and context
Empowerment	From directing to developing	Hand back responsibility with trust

Together, they create what I call **The Coaching Triangle of Transformation** — each side reinforcing the other to create growth that lasts.

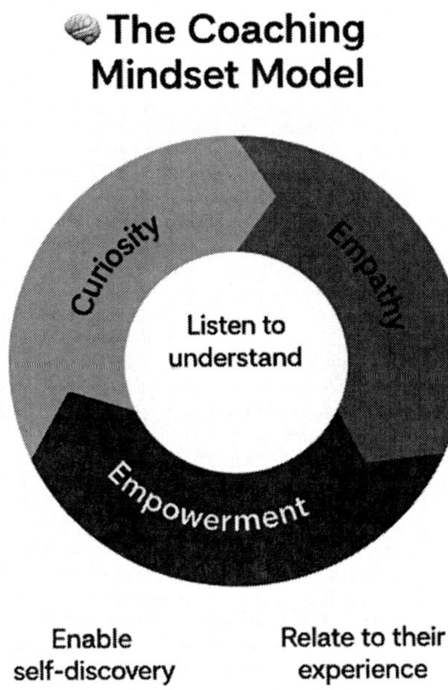

Figure 6: The Coaching Mindset Model — Curiosity → Empathy → Empowerment

Coaching begins with curiosity, deepens through empathy, and leads to empowerment — enabling awareness, confidence, and growth.

Curiosity – The Doorway to Awareness

Curiosity is the opposite of assumption. It's the courage to not know — and still stay present.

Gary Kirsten, the South African coach who guided India to the 2011 World Cup victory, often said:

"My job was not to teach Sachin Tendulkar how to bat. It was to ask the questions that made him reflect."

He approached coaching with a learner's mindset. Every player was unique; his role was to *discover* their rhythm, not impose one.

In one interview, he said:

"Coaching is 80% listening, 20% guidance. Players already have answers — you just help them hear them."

Corporate reflection: Before giving advice, ask — *"What do you think would work?"*

Empathy – The Bridge of Trust

Empathy is not sympathy. It's not "feeling for" someone — it's "feeling with" them.

When Anil Kumble took over as India's coach in 2016, he brought the same analytical precision he'd shown as a bowler. But he also led with heart.

During one overseas tour, a young player was struggling. Kumble didn't lecture him. He invited him for dinner, listened quietly, and said:

"You're not alone in this. We've all been there."

That night didn't just rebuild confidence — it rebuilt trust.

In corporate life, too, empathy transforms culture. Teams don't remember what you said; they remember how you made them feel when they failed.

Empowerment – The Final Leap

Empowerment is where curiosity and empathy become action. It's when you say, *"I trust you to figure it out."*

One of the most powerful examples comes again from Gopichand. When P.V. Sindhu prepared for the Rio Olympics, he told her:

"I can guide you to the court. But once you step in, it's your game."

He didn't micromanage; he mentored. That trust turned into silver — and eventually gold.

In organizations, empowerment looks like:

- Delegating with clarity, not control.
- Trusting intent over perfection.
- Celebrating learning, not just outcomes.

Reflection Practice – The 3R Model (Self-Coaching)

When faced with a challenge, try:

Reflect: What am I feeling and why?

Reframe: What else could be true here?

Respond: What's the best next action aligned to my values?

This simple model builds self-coaching muscle — the foundation of every great Coach.

The Science Behind Coaching

Neuroscience shows that when people find their own solutions, dopamine levels rise, creating positive reinforcement. That's why insight lasts longer than instruction.

Coaching literally rewires the brain for ownership and resilience.

We've seen how Gopichand, Kirsten, and Kumble embody the three core pillars of coaching. But how do you translate these principles into everyday leadership?

In the next section, we'll explore the **Coaching Conversation Framework** — a step-by-step guide to turn every dialogue into a moment of growth — and learn how leaders build coaching cultures where potential becomes performance.

The Coaching Mindset in Action: Turning Conversations into Transformation

From Dialogue to Discovery

A coaching conversation is not a talk between a superior and a subordinate; it's a *shared exploration* between two learners. The Coach's role is to create a *thinking space* — where silence works as power, curiosity fuels clarity, and awareness becomes action.

As Gary Kirsten once said after India's 2011 World Cup win:

"I never told players what to do. I simply helped them think clearly and trust themselves more."

That's the essence of coaching in action — **clarity over control**.

The Coaching Conversation Framework

Every great coaching moment moves through a natural rhythm — I call it the **G-R-O-W-T-H Loop**.

Step	Purpose	Coach's Cue	Example Question
G – Goal	Clarify what success looks like	Set direction	"What outcome would make this conversation valuable for you?"
R – Reality	Understand what's happening now	Explore facts & feelings	"What's working well? What's challenging?"
O – Options	Expand perspective	Invite possibilities	"What choices do you see?"
W – Will	Strengthen commitment	Confirm intent	"Which option feels right to act on first?"
T – Tactics	Design small next steps	Plan forward	"What specific action will you take this week?"
H – Habits	Reinforce the learning loop	Sustain momentum	"What habit would keep this progress alive?"

This structure keeps conversations focused, future-oriented, and empowering.

Story – Gary Kirsten and Dhoni: Trust Over Tactics

When Gary Kirsten took charge as coach of the Indian cricket team in 2008, the team was talented yet fragmented after internal transitions. He realized early: *he didn't need to teach them cricket — he needed to create trust.*

He began with one-to-ones, not team speeches. He asked every player:

"What does success mean to you personally, and how can I support that?"

That question changed the dynamic. Instead of giving orders, he gave ownership.

Under his coaching, India rose to become World No. 1 in Tests and World Cup champions — not by domination, but by **dialogue**.

His partnership with M.S. Dhoni became legendary because both valued humility and authenticity over hierarchy. Kirsten later said:

"Dhoni didn't need me to lead him. He needed me to believe in him."

Corporate Parallel

A similar transformation happened with a leader I coached in a multinational bank. She began replacing directives with questions. Within a quarter, her team's initiative scores shot up. She told me,

"When I stopped answering everything, people started thinking again."

That's the *Kirsten effect*—when belief becomes performance.

Anil Kumble – The Coach Who Listened With Data and Heart

Anil Kumble, India's former test captain and later coach, brought a rare mix of analytical precision and deep empathy. He'd arrive at review sessions with meticulous notes but begin with one question:

"How are you feeling about your game right now?"

He called this *emotional analytics* — combining numbers with narratives.

When a player struggled, he didn't start with form; he started with *focus*. He believed that *listening is a strategy*.

That blend of science and sensitivity defines modern coaching — **head meets heart**.

The Corporate Lesson

Great coaches use data to inform, not define. Metrics matter, but meaning motivates. Before quoting KPIs, begin by understanding the person behind them.

Everyday Coaching Moments

Coaching doesn't require a scheduled session. It happens in *micro-moments* — hallway chats, project reviews, or casual check-ins.

Try these three simple practices:

1. **Pause Before Response** – When someone brings a problem, breathe before answering. The pause signals respect.
2. **Ask One Powerful Question** – Replace "Here's what you should do" with "What do you think would work best?"
3. **Reflect Back** – Summarise what you heard: "So, you're aiming to …, and what's holding you back is …?"

Each small shift builds a culture of reflection.

From Feedback to Feed-Forward

Traditional feedback looks backward — what went wrong. Coaching-style *feed-forward* looks ahead — what's next.

Marshall Goldsmith, the executive coach who's worked with over 100 CEOs, says:

"We can't change the past, but we can create the future."

Instead of "You missed the target," say:

"What can we tweak next time to get there faster?"

Feedback corrects; feed-forward develops.

The Listening Spectrum

Coaches listen on three levels:

Level	Focus	Example of Presence
1 – Internal	Your own thoughts while others talk	"How will I reply?"
2 – Focused	The speaker's words and tone	"What exactly are they saying?"
3 – Global	Emotions, pauses, environment	"What's being felt or unsaid?"

Mastering Level 3 listening builds empathy and trust instantly.

Practice – The Coaching Micro-Routine

At the end of each day, note one conversation where you could have:

- Asked more than advised,
- Listened longer than you spoke,
- Reflected instead of reacted.

Small awareness, repeated daily, turns leadership into coaching.

Reflection Questions

1. When was the last time I truly listened without planning my reply?
2. How often do I ask questions that make others think deeper?
3. What does empowerment look like in my daily leadership?
4. Do people leave my conversations more confident or more dependent?

5. How could I bring more curiosity and patience into tomorrow's interactions?

By now, you've seen coaching as both a mindset and a method. The next section will take it one level higher — showing how **coaching becomes culture**. We'll explore how organizations like TATA Group, Infosys Leadership Institute, and sports ecosystems such as the Indian Hockey Federation use coaching to build *collective excellence*. We'll also close with *The Coach's Credo* — your daily declaration of growth, empathy, and empowerment.

Building a Coaching Culture & The Coach's Credo

From Coaching Conversations to Coaching Culture

Coaching begins with one leader asking better questions. But true transformation begins when *everyone* in an organization learns to listen, reflect, and empower.

It's when "What went wrong?" becomes "What can we learn?" It's when feedback becomes fuel, and reflection becomes rhythm.

That's when coaching stops being a skill — and becomes a **culture**.

A Story from the Field

A few years ago, I worked with a global consulting firm that wanted to embed coaching as part of leadership DNA. Initially, managers saw coaching as something "HR does." But after several experiential sessions, one senior director said something profound:

"I realized coaching isn't another meeting. It's a way of being in every conversation."

Within six months, the company saw visible changes:

- 360° feedback scores improved.
- Attrition dropped.
- Internal promotions increased.

Why? Because when leaders coach, people don't just perform — they **grow**.

What Makes a Coaching Culture?

Organizations with strong coaching cultures share four common features. I call it the **4C Framework** — simple, actionable, and sustainable.

Pillar	Focus	Example in Action
Clarity	Everyone knows what coaching *means* in their context.	Define coaching values & boundaries (not therapy, not telling).
Capability	Leaders are equipped with coaching skills.	Workshops on listening, feedback, and questioning.

Consistency	Coaching becomes part of rhythms & rituals.	1:1 check-ins, peer coaching, and learning circles.
Commitment	Leadership models it visibly.	Senior leaders practice coaching publicly & reward it.

Culture doesn't shift through memos. It shifts through **modeling**. Every time a leader listens deeply, asks curiously, and empowers consciously, the culture evolves.

Corporate Example – Infosys Leadership Institute

Infosys built a world-class leadership pipeline by integrating coaching as a leadership competency. Their philosophy: *"Leaders create leaders."*

Every manager receives coaching training, and every senior leader sponsors at least one internal coach. The result? A culture where growth conversations are part of daily rhythm — not annual reviews.

In the words of a senior HR leader:

"When people feel coached, they feel cared for. That's what drives engagement."

The Ripple Effect – From Self to System

When one leader learns to coach, a ripple begins.

→ Self-awareness improves communication.

→ Communication strengthens relationships.

→ Relationships elevate performance.

→ Performance shapes culture.

That's how a single shift in *how we talk* changes *how we work.*

It's what happened when Gary Kirsten coached Dhoni, when Gopichand coached Sindhu, when Anil Kumble mentored India's youth — **one conversation at a time**.

In corporate life, too, transformation doesn't come from strategy decks. It comes from *moments of presence.*

A 15-minute reflection call. A single empathetic question. A pause before advice.

Culture grows through repetition of care.

The Coach as Catalyst

Coaches act as mirrors — not magnifiers. They don't inflate egos; they illuminate awareness.

In the organizational context, coaching leaders help teams:

- Move from compliance to commitment.
- Replace competition with collaboration.
- Transform performance into purpose.

A senior leader at a Global Company once told me:

"When I started coaching my people, I realized I was also coaching myself."

That's the secret — coaching others is the fastest way to grow your own self-awareness.

From Skill to Spirit

Many leaders ask, *"Can anyone be a coach?"* The answer is yes — if you cultivate three inner qualities:

1. **Presence** – Being fully in the moment without distraction.
2. **Patience** – Allowing silence and reflection without rushing.
3. **Partnership** – Seeing others as equal thinkers, not subordinates.

The outer tools matter, but the inner stance sustains. The Coach's true gift isn't their knowledge — it's their **belief in human potential**.

The Coach's Credo – The Declaration of Growth

At the end of every workshop, I often share this with leaders — a daily reminder of what it means to live as a coach.

The Coach's Credo

I choose curiosity over certainty. I listen not to reply, but to reveal. I ask questions that unlock thought, and silence that awakens insight.

I trust in potential more than position. I believe every person is capable, creative, and complete — just waiting to be seen.

I give feedback with compassion, and challenge with care.

I celebrate effort, not just outcome. I create space where others grow — and in doing so, I grow too.

I coach not to change people, but to help them discover who they already are.

This credo isn't meant to be read — it's meant to be *lived.* Frame it. Keep it on your desk. Or reflect on one line each morning before your first meeting.

The Inner Evolution of the Corporate Athlete

As you've now seen —

- The *Player* performs.
- The *Captain* leads.
- The *Coach* transforms.

Each phase builds on the last, creating a complete performance cycle — from *self-mastery to shared mastery.*

Coaching represents the highest evolution of leadership — where your legacy lives in the growth of others.

Just as Gopichand produced champions, and Rahul Dravid now shapes India's cricketing future, your greatest impact won't be in what you achieve, but in *who you help others become.*

Closing Reflection – The Mirror of Growth

Pause for a moment. Reflect quietly on these questions:

1. Who has been a "coach" in my life — someone who believed in me before I did?
2. How can I pay that forward in my team, family, or community?
3. What one behavior could make me a more empowering leader tomorrow?

Because coaching isn't a title — it's a legacy of belief.

You've now mastered the outer and inner game of leadership. But even the most skilled players, captains, and coaches face the toughest opponent — *themselves.*

The next chapter explores the world within — **Mindset, Resilience, and Renewal.** You'll discover how elite performers sustain focus and flow through adversity, and how Corporate Athletes can do the same in the boardroom and beyond.

KEY TAKEAWAYS – CHAPTER 5

- ☑ Coaching is a mindset of curiosity, empathy, and empowerment.
- ☑ Great leaders grow others through reflection, not direction.
- ☑ Coaching cultures thrive through clarity, capability, consistency, and commitment.
- ☑ The best leaders measure success not by control, but by the confidence they create.
- ☑ Coaching transforms performance into purpose — and people into possibilities.

"The best coaches don't change people — they create the space where people change themselves."

Chapter 6

MINDSET, RESILIENCE, AND RENEWAL – THE INNER GAME OF THE CORPORATE ATHLETE

Training the Mind for Clarity, Confidence, and Consistency

"Champions are not those who never fail — they are those who recover fast, reflect deep, and return stronger."

The Inner Game: Mastering Mindset

The Arena Within

Every athlete trains two games — the *outer* game of skills and the *inner* game of mind. The outer game wins medals. The inner game sustains mastery.

Corporate life mirrors this truth. We can master strategy, process, and performance, but if we lose emotional balance, fatigue, fear, or self-doubt takes over — the game is lost from within.

Success in today's world is not about *more effort*; it's about *mental alignment.*

The mind is your ultimate muscle — and mindset is your training ground.

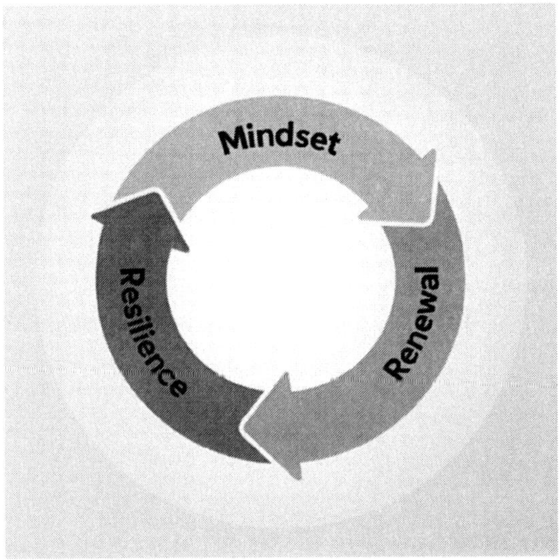

Figure 7: The Inner Game Model — Mindset Resilience Renewal

True performance begins within — when we align our thoughts, emotions, and energy toward purposeful renewal.

Abhinav Bindra: Precision, Pressure, and Presence

Abhinav Bindra — India's first individual Olympic gold medalist — exemplifies mastery of the inner game. Shooting, unlike many sports, leaves no room for adrenaline or aggression. It's about stillness, precision, and presence under immense pressure.

Bindra once said:

"In shooting, 99% is the mind. The trigger is only 1%."

He trained his focus relentlessly — not just on targets, but on thoughts. He simulated failure deliberately in practice: lights flickering, crowd noise, unexpected interruptions — all to test emotional control.

What he discovered:

"Winning is not about hitting the bullseye. It's about managing the mind before the shot."

That's what mindset mastery is — managing emotion before execution.

Corporate Reflection:

In the corporate arena, this is the art of staying calm before a high-stakes meeting, a client pitch, or a tough review. Your version of the "bullseye" might be a deadline, a presentation, or a conversation with your boss. The secret is to build inner rituals that stabilize focus.

Try this:

- **Before performance:** Breathe deeply for 60 seconds.
- **During performance:** Focus on the *process*, not the outcome.
- **After performance:** Reflect, don't react.

That's your mental gym.

Mary Kom: The Power of Purpose

While Bindra's arena was silent, Mary Kom's was full of noise — punches, pressure, and prejudice. As a woman boxer from

Manipur, she faced not only opponents in the ring but stereotypes outside it.

Her story isn't just about physical strength; it's about mental endurance. Returning to world-class boxing after motherhood, she trained at dawn, cared for her twins, and fought her way to a historic Olympic medal.

When asked what kept her going, she said simply:

"My purpose was bigger than my pain."

Purpose transforms endurance into excellence.

Corporate Reflection:

Pressure is inevitable. What changes is your *perspective.* If your work is connected to purpose — personal or collective — fatigue becomes fuel.

When you remember *why* you're doing something, the *how* takes care of itself.

As a Corporate Athlete, align every performance goal with a deeper purpose — the value or contribution that fuels it.

Mindset Practices for Professionals

Practice	Purpose	Example
Visualization	Create mental rehearsal before action	Picture the ideal outcome of a meeting or project.

Practice	Purpose	Example
Anchoring	Stabilize emotional state	Use a deep breath, gesture, or keyword ("calm", "clarity") before a stressful task.
Reflection	Build awareness post-performance	Journal key insights after major presentations or decisions.

These are not soft skills — they are *focus frameworks.* They train the mind to operate in clarity instead of chaos.

Mindset prepares the mind. Resilience protects the spirit.

Next, we'll explore how great performers — like Saina Nehwal and Rahul Dravid — bounce back from defeat, redefine failure, and build emotional strength that sustains over time.

The Art of Resilience: Learning to Fall and Rise

Resilience Is a Skill, Not a Trait

Many people assume resilience is something you're born with — like talent. It isn't. It's built through *reflection, repetition, and reframing.*

Resilience is the ability to face a challenge, learn from it, and come back stronger. It's the muscle that turns stress into strength.

Saina Nehwal: The Comeback Code

Saina Nehwal's story is not just of victories but of *rebounds.* After achieving a world #1 ranking, injuries nearly ended her career. The pressure was immense — media scrutiny, expectations, and physical pain.

But she turned recovery into training. She used her rehab period not just to rebuild her body, but to reset her mindset.

"Every injury taught me to respect the body and listen to it," she said.

That humility — not toughness — became her strength.

When she returned to international tournaments, her game was leaner, sharper, and mentally tougher. That's resilience — bouncing *forward*, not just *back*.

Rahul Dravid: The Gentleman's Resilience

Known as "The Wall," Rahul Dravid symbolizes quiet consistency. He wasn't the most flamboyant, but he was the most *reliable.*

His greatness wasn't built on power — it was built on preparation and patience. When critics doubted his ability in one-day cricket, he didn't argue. He adapted — reinventing his role as a wicketkeeper-batsman for the team's cause.

He once said:

"You can't control results. You can only control your response."

That's the essence of mental resilience — detaching identity from outcome.

Corporate Reflection:

Every setback at work — a lost client, missed goal, or tough feedback — is a "training net." The goal isn't to avoid it, but to *bounce forward.*

Try this **3-Step Rebound Routine:**

1. **Pause** – Acknowledge emotion without judgment.
2. **Perspective** – Ask, "What is this trying to teach me?"
3. **Plan** – Identify one improvement for next time.

Resilience isn't about ignoring pain. It's about *transforming* it into progress.

The Science of Recovery

Sports psychology calls this the **Stress–Recovery Loop.**

When we experience stress, the body releases cortisol. If we don't recover, fatigue compounds — leading to burnout. But when we build deliberate recovery rituals — rest, reflection, exercise, silence — we restore focus and resilience.

High-performing professionals need *recovery as much as readiness.*

The Flow Zone

Resilient professionals often find what Mihaly Csikszentmihalyi called *flow* — the state where skill and challenge meet perfectly. In flow, you lose track of time, self-consciousness fades, and performance becomes effortless.

Athletes call it "the zone." In corporate life, it happens when your work stretches you just enough to stay engaged — not overwhelmed.

To cultivate flow:

- Minimize distractions.
- Work in focused time blocks (90–120 minutes).
- Take mindful breaks.

Resilience helps you rise. Renewal helps you *sustain.*

Renewal and Flow: Sustaining Long-Term Peak Performance

The Recovery Myth

Most professionals push harder when tired — believing effort alone ensures success. Athletes know better: recovery is *part* of performance.

Elite performers schedule rest with the same discipline as training. Recovery isn't laziness — it's maintenance.

Bindra called it *mental tuning.* Gopichand called it *active rest.* You should call it *leadership hygiene.*

The Renewal Cycle

True performance follows this natural rhythm: **Exertion → Reflection → Renewal → Reinvention**

Phase	Focus	Action
Exertion	High effort	Deliver, perform, stretch
Reflection	Awareness	Review, learn, course-correct
Renewal	Recovery	Rest, disconnect, nourish
Reinvention	Growth	Apply learning and evolve

When leaders skip renewal, they sabotage reinvention.

The Rituals of Renewal

Borrowed from sports and adapted for corporate life, these rituals sustain excellence:

1. **Micro Recovery:** 5-minute pauses between meetings to reset breathing.
2. **Weekly Reflection:** Journal top three wins and one lesson.
3. **Digital Detox:** 1 day each week without work-related screens.
4. **Physical Practice:** Consistent movement — yoga, walking, or stretching.
5. **Mental Nutrition:** Reading, silence, or prayer to replenish the mind.

Renewal protects purpose.

Corporate Case – The Resilient Organization

One of India's largest IT companies introduced *"Mindful Mondays"* — 15 minutes of silence before the week begins. Initially, leaders found it awkward. Within a few months, engagement and focus improved measurably.

Quiet time became a collective recharge — turning mindfulness into a performance advantage.

The Inner Balance

At the highest level, performance is no longer about doing more — it's about doing meaningfully.

As a Corporate Athlete, your real success is measured by balance — between ambition and awareness, discipline and detachment, striving and serenity.

The Mindset Loop

Here's the full cycle every Corporate Athlete must master:

Mindset → Resilience → Renewal → Mastery → Mindset (again)

Each phase feeds the next — creating sustainable growth. This is the loop of long-term excellence.

Closing Reflection

Pause and reflect on these:

1. What drains me — and what renews me?
2. How do I respond under pressure — reactively or reflectively?
3. What's one renewal ritual I can begin this week?
4. How can I shift from managing time to managing energy?

Because energy, not hours, defines performance.

KEY TAKEAWAYS

- ☑ Mindset mastery is the foundation of consistent excellence.
- ☑ Resilience is built through awareness and recovery, not avoidance.
- ☑ Renewal sustains purpose, clarity, and emotional strength.
- ☑ Flow emerges when skill and challenge are in harmony.
- ☑ The inner game always precedes the outer result.

"You don't build resilience by avoiding struggle — you build it by finding meaning within it."

Chapter 7

PURPOSE AND PEAK PERFORMANCE – PLAYING THE INFINITE GAME

Finding Meaning, Motivation, and Mastery in the Corporate Arena

"When your work connects with your purpose, excellence becomes effortless."

From Winning to Meaning: Redefining Success

The Paradox of Achievement

The higher you climb, the quieter the applause becomes. Every peak reached reveals another. And yet, many who reach the top describe a strange emptiness — not failure, but *fatigue of meaning.*

Athletes face it after championships. Executives face it after decades of striving. The question silently arises — *what now?*

The answer lies in playing the **Infinite Game**.

Finite vs. Infinite Game

In a finite game, the goal is to win. In an infinite game, the goal is to continue growing, contributing, and evolving.

Finite Game	Infinite Game
Win at any cost	Grow with every challenge
Compete against others	Improve upon yourself
Celebrate outcomes	Celebrate progress
Chase success	Create significance

The Corporate Athlete's greatest transition is from *achievement* to *alignment* — from chasing outcomes to living purpose.

Sachin Tendulkar: Beyond the Scoreboard

Sachin Tendulkar's career spanned 24 years — a lifetime of peaks, pressure, and performance. But what defined him wasn't just records. It was *renewal through purpose.*

After every century, he'd reset. After every injury, he'd return. After every criticism, he'd reflect.

He said in his farewell speech:

"I played for my country, my team, and my people. That gave me strength when my body had none."

His purpose was larger than the pitch. And that's why his performance sustained through decades — it was fuelled by *service*, not just *success.*

Corporate Reflection:

When your "why" becomes about contribution — customers, community, or cause — your energy multiplies. Purpose becomes your renewable energy source.

In a meeting, project, or decision, ask yourself:

"How does this contribute — not just to results, but to people?"

That one question shifts work from *effort* to *expression.*

Discovering Your Purpose through Ikigai

The Essence of Ikigai

The Japanese concept of **Ikigai** means *"reason for being."* It sits at the intersection of:

- What you love
- What you're good at
- What the world needs
- What you can be paid for

When these four align, work becomes meaningful, and performance becomes joyful.

Figure 8: The Corporate Ikigai Model — Aligning Purpose and Performance

Sustainable success emerges when your passion, talent, service, and value intersect — creating flow, meaning, and fulfillment.

PV Sindhu: Passion Meets Purpose

PV Sindhu's rise wasn't just talent — it was *intentional purpose alignment.* Her love for badminton met her discipline, her skills met her country's needs, and her contribution inspired millions.

After winning Olympic silver, she could have slowed down. Instead, she said:

"I don't play for medals. I play to make India proud every single time."

That's Ikigai in motion — purpose driving performance.

Your Corporate Ikigai Reflection

Take 15 minutes to answer these:

1. What activities make you feel alive and energized?
2. What skills come naturally to you?
3. What needs in your organization or community resonate with you?
4. How can your work create sustainable value — financial, social, or emotional?

Where these overlap — that's your **Corporate Ikigai Zone**.

Corporate Example – Ratan Tata: The Infinite Game of Impact

Ratan Tata's leadership philosophy perfectly captures the Infinite Game mindset. He once said:

"I don't believe in making the right decisions. I make decisions and make them right."

For Tata, business was never just profit; it was *purpose with impact.* From affordable mobility (Tata Nano) to global ethics, his decisions were guided by legacy, not quarterly numbers.

He played the infinite game — building trust that outlasts trends.

The Purpose–Performance Loop

Purpose doesn't compete with performance — it *feeds* it.

Here's the loop every Corporate Athlete must nurture:

Purpose → Energy → Performance → Fulfilment → Deeper Purpose

Each feeds the next. When purpose fuels action, performance feels natural. When performance brings fulfillment, purpose deepens.

This is the self-sustaining rhythm of the infinite player.

The Science of Purpose and Motivation

The Neuroscience of Meaning

Research in neuroscience shows that working with a sense of purpose activates the brain's *dopamine* and *serotonin* systems — increasing motivation, focus, and resilience.

Purpose also engages the *prefrontal cortex*, the brain's decision-making center — helping you stay calm and strategic under stress.

That's why people aligned with purpose don't burn out easily. They may tire physically, but not emotionally — because their "why" keeps the fire alive.

Corporate Insight:

In a study by McKinsey (2022), employees who found purpose at work were:

- 2.4× more engaged,
- 3× more likely to stay longer, and
- 5× more likely to describe work as fulfilling.

Purpose, therefore, isn't poetic — it's *profitable.*

The Three Levels of Purpose

Level	Focus	Key Question
Personal	Inner meaning and values	"What gives my work meaning?"
Professional	Excellence in craft	"How does my work make a difference?"
Collective	Shared mission	"How does our team or organization improve lives?"

When all three align, individuals move from pressure to passion — from stress to flow.

Playing the Infinite Game

The Infinite Mindset Framework

Simon Sinek's research on the Infinite Game reveals five practices that help leaders and organizations thrive through uncertainty. Let's adapt them for the Corporate Athlete.

Practice	Meaning	Corporate Athlete Application
Just Cause	Serve a purpose beyond profit.	Define your "why" clearly in every role.

Trusting Teams	Create psychological safety.	Build honest, feedback-rich relationships.
Worthy Rival	Learn from competition.	Compete to grow, not to dominate.
Existential Flexibility	Adapt when your purpose demands it.	Be willing to reinvent your playbook.
Courage to Lead	Act with integrity even under pressure.	Make values visible through choices.

When you play infinitely, setbacks become teachers, not threats.

Sports Parallels – Dhoni's Calm and Kohli's Drive

Dhoni represents *infinite calm* — detached focus, composure, and adaptability. Kohli represents *infinite drive* — constant reinvention, hunger for excellence, and love for the process.

Both complement each other. One leads with peace, the other with passion — and both play for *progress*, not just *prizes.*

The modern Corporate Athlete must cultivate both calm for clarity, drive for direction.

The Legacy Lens

Purpose naturally extends into legacy — not what you leave *behind*, but what you leave *within* others.

Think of Rahul Dravid coaching India's U-19 team — instilling discipline, humility, and self-belief. Or Narayana Murthy mentoring leaders who carried forward Infosys values.

Legacy is the echo of your purpose in other people's lives.

The Purpose Practice

Here's a weekly reflection ritual to keep purpose active:

1. **Sunday Reset:** Revisit your "why." Why does your work matter this week?
2. **Midweek Check-In:** Ask, "Am I operating from ambition or alignment?"
3. **Friday Review:** Note one moment where you felt truly alive in your work — that's your purpose in action.

Purpose must be practiced, not proclaimed.

The Renewal Connection

Purpose also restores energy — it's your emotional recharge. When you feel drained, revisit your "why." You'll find that meaning, not caffeine, is the ultimate fuel.

Story – The Executive Who Found His "Why"

Arjun, a senior leader at a Fortune 500 firm, had reached what he thought was success — position, perks, prestige. Yet he felt empty.

Through coaching, we uncovered that his true joy came from mentoring young talent. He redefined his career mission:

"To help people grow faster than they believe possible."

That shift changed everything. His performance improved, his stress reduced, and his team thrived. He wasn't chasing success anymore — he was *living significance.*

Closing Reflections: Purpose as Practice

At the summit of performance lies simplicity. When your actions align with purpose, leadership becomes effortless.

"The Infinite Player wakes up each day not to prove, but to improve."

Purpose is not a destination. It's a daily decision — a compass that keeps you aligned in chaos.

When you play the infinite game, you stop measuring life by milestones and start experiencing it through meaning.

Reflection Prompts

1. What gives your work meaning — beyond metrics?
2. How do you define success in your current role?
3. Whose life improves because you do what you do?
4. What would "playing the infinite game" look like for you this year?
5. How will you measure legacy — not in outcomes, but in impact?

KEY TAKEAWAYS

- ☑ Purpose fuels sustainable performance.
- ☑ Ikigai aligns passion, skill, service, and value.
- ☑ The Infinite Game mindset transforms work into contribution.
- ☑ Legacy is not what you achieve, but who you elevate.
- ☑ When you work with meaning, you win even when you don't "win."

"Your Ikigai is where your passion meets your purpose, your skill meets service, and your work meets meaning."

Chapter 8

THE RIPPLE EFFECT OF COACHING: FROM SELF TO CULTURE

From Personal Growth to Collective Excellence

"When one person is coached, a life changes. When an organization embraces coaching, a culture transforms."

From Self Mastery to Systemic Growth

By now, we've explored the *inner journey* of the Corporate Athlete — from the **Player's discipline**, the **Captain's vision**, and the **Coach's empathy**, to **Purpose and Peak Performance**.

But the story doesn't end with personal mastery. True transformation begins when personal growth turns into *collective evolution.*

It's when leadership becomes legacy, and reflection becomes rhythm.

When teams start coaching each other — not because they're told to, but because they've *seen what it does to energy, trust, and performance* — that's when culture changes.

The Ripple Effect

Every great transformation starts small. One reflective question. One act of listening. One conversation that shifts from judgment to curiosity.

Over time, these moments ripple outward — from individuals to teams, from teams to the organization, and from the organization to society.

That's the **Ripple Effect of Coaching™**.

Coaching starts as a conversation, but it ends as a culture.

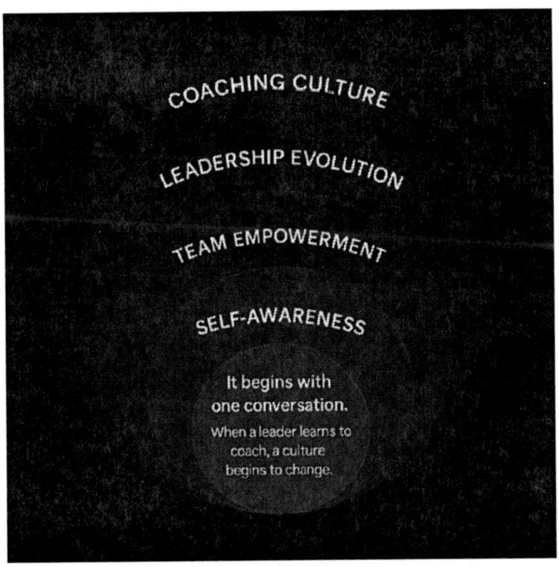

Figure 9: The Ripple effect of Coaching

Transformation begins within individuals but multiplies through relationships, teams, organizations.

The Coaching Advantage in the Modern Workplace

In today's world of hybrid teams, generational diversity, AI disruption, and relentless speed — people don't just want to be managed. They want to be *mentored, empowered, and trusted.*

Traditional management (command–control–comply) is giving way to coaching-based leadership (connect–coach–collaborate).

The Coaching Advantage

According to the **ICF Global Coaching Study (2023):**

- 86% of organizations with coaching cultures report higher engagement,
- 70% show stronger collaboration and communication, and
- 60% see measurable gains in performance and well-being.

Coaching works because it addresses the *whole person*, not just the performer.

Corporate Case – Hindustan Unilever (HUL)

At HUL, managers undergo "Leader as Coach" training as part of their leadership curriculum. The focus isn't only on performance conversations — but *growth conversations.*

Leaders are taught to ask three simple questions in every 1:1:

1. What are you learning right now?
2. What's helping you grow?

3. What's holding you back?

These micro-moments of curiosity have reshaped HUL's leadership pipeline — building reflection, trust, and ownership.

From Command to Coaching: The New Leadership Shift

Old Paradigm vs. New Paradigm

Managing	Coaching
Directive	Developmental
Controls decisions	Enables thinking
Gives answers	Asks questions
Evaluates performance	Expands potential
Focuses on metrics	Focuses on meaning

The coaching mindset represents *evolutionary leadership* — from commanding outcomes to cultivating awareness.

Story: The Leader Who Chose to Listen

Ravi, a senior project head in a technology company, was known for being a "driver." His teams delivered, but morale dipped.

In a coaching workshop, he realized he'd been leading through urgency, not empathy. He decided to change one habit — instead of opening meetings with "updates," he began with "How are you doing this week?"

In three months, productivity went *up*, stress went *down*, and team retention improved. He said,

"I didn't change the process — I changed the presence."

That's the power of coaching in action — small shifts that create big waves.

The 4C Framework for Building a Coaching Culture

To transform organizations sustainably, leaders can apply the **4C Framework** — the practical architecture for embedding coaching into corporate DNA.

Pillar	Focus	Example in Practice
Clarity	Define what coaching means for the organization.	Create a "Coaching Charter" aligning leaders to shared principles.
Capability	Build coaching skills at every level.	Conduct internal training & peer-coaching circles.
Consistency	Integrate coaching into everyday rituals.	Embed reflective questions in reviews, meetings, and stand-ups.
Commitment	Model coaching from the top.	Senior leaders share personal coaching stories.

Culture doesn't change through announcements — it changes through *embodiment.* When leaders listen deeply, question curiously, and empower intentionally, they model what they wish to multiply.

Corporate Example – Infosys Leadership Institute

Infosys' **Leadership Institute (ILI)** has long been recognized for embedding *coaching and mentoring* into its leadership philosophy. Their guiding belief is simple: **"Leaders create leaders."**

At Infosys, leadership development is not limited to skills training — it's built on reflection, feedback, and internal coaching. Senior leaders are encouraged to *coach and mentor emerging talent*, creating a culture of continuous learning and empowerment.

Over the years, this approach has strengthened engagement, enhanced leadership depth, and contributed to a sustainable pipeline of future-ready managers.

Infosys realized that **coaching is not a cost — it's a multiplier**. It amplifies trust, accelerates learning, and anchors performance in purpose.

Coaching at the Systemic Level

From Individuals to Ecosystems

Organizations that sustain coaching cultures go beyond one-on-one sessions. They build **coaching ecosystems** — interconnected systems of support, feedback, and growth.

These include:

- **Manager-as-Coach** training.
- **Peer coaching circles.**
- **Reflective learning communities.**
- **Executive coaching partnerships.**

Each node reinforces the culture of awareness and accountability.

"When reflection becomes ritual, growth becomes inevitable."

Case Insight: Tata Group's Coaching Culture

Tata Group has long been admired for its deep commitment to values-driven leadership and people development. In recent years, the Group has steadily integrated *coaching conversations* into its leadership philosophy — emphasizing empathy, reflection, and collaboration across its diverse companies.

Through initiatives like "Leaders as Coaches" and ongoing leadership development programs, Tata leaders are encouraged to move beyond managing tasks to *developing people.* This shift reflects a larger Tata ethos — that leadership is not about control, but about creating space for others to grow.

As one senior HR leader from the Group expressed in a public forum:

"We moved from asking, *'What's the plan?'* to asking, *'What's the learning?'* — and everything changed."

Today, coaching is seen within Tata not as an external intervention but as an *everyday leadership behavior* — cultivating purpose-driven, self-aware, and collaborative executives across generations.

The Ripple Effect of Coaching

Let's visualize how coaching transforms performance — not linearly, but exponentially.

🌊 The Ripple Effect of Coaching

Level	Focus	Transformation
Self	Awareness and reflection	Greater clarity, emotional balance, focus
Team	Trust and feedback	Stronger relationships, collaboration, ownership
Organization	Shared learning	Culture of openness, adaptability, and innovation
Society	Leadership by example	Ethical, conscious, and human-centered growth

When coaching becomes the way people *think*, not just a tool they *use*, organizations evolve from **performance machines** to **learning ecosystems.**

Sports Parallel – Gopichand's Coaching Philosophy

Pullela Gopichand, India's national badminton coach, is a living example of the Ripple Effect. He not only produced world champions like PV Sindhu and Saina Nehwal but also built a *system* that nurtures future champions.

His coaching philosophy:

"Discipline creates excellence, but values sustain it."

He built an academy where athletes learn humility, nutrition, mindfulness, and reflection — not just skills. That's how transformation scales — when excellence becomes collective.

The Coaching Leader's Toolkit

Here are five everyday coaching practices for leaders to embed in their teams:

1. **Ask Before Advising:** "What do you think might work here?" → Builds ownership and confidence.
2. **Reflect Together:** End meetings with, "What did we learn today?" → Turns results into wisdom.
3. **Appreciate Effort, Not Just Outcomes:** → Reinforces growth mindset.
4. **Model Curiosity:** → Show vulnerability by saying, "I don't have all the answers — what do you think?"
5. **Pause for Presence:** → Take 60 seconds of silence before decision-making meetings.

Small practices. Massive impact.

The ROI of Coaching

Research confirms what intuition already knows: Coaching doesn't just build better people — it builds better results.

- **80%** of coaching clients report improved self-confidence.
- **73%** report improved relationships.
- **67%** report better work–life balance. *(ICF Global Study, 2022)*

For organizations, this translates into:

- Lower attrition.
- Higher innovation.
- Stronger culture.

The **real ROI** of coaching is *trust.* And trust is the foundation of transformation.

Practice: The 3A Habit

Try the **3A Coaching Habit**™ for 21 days:

1. **Ask** — one meaningful question daily that deepens reflection.
2. **Acknowledge** — one genuine appreciation for effort or insight.
3. **Allow** — one moment of silence before responding, to create space.

Within weeks, conversations shift from transactional to transformational.

The Coach's Legacy

In the end, the role of a leader–coach is not to create followers — it's to create more leaders. That's what coaching achieves: it multiplies maturity.

Think of it this way:

- The **Player** wins games.
- The **Captain** builds teams.
- The **Coach** builds generations.

That's the future of leadership.

Closing Reflection

Pause and ask yourself:

1. How do I show up in my conversations — to direct or to develop?
2. What's one coaching habit I can bring to my next meeting?
3. How might I help someone find their voice this week?

Remember: leadership is not about control — it's about creating conditions where people can flourish.

"When you coach others, you awaken the leader within yourself."

KEY TAKEAWAYS

☑ Coaching transforms individuals, teams, and culture.

☑ The 4C Framework — Clarity, Capability, Consistency, Commitment — drives sustainable growth.

☑ The Ripple Effect of Coaching™ spreads from Self → Team → Organization → Society.

☑ The ROI of coaching is not just productivity — it's purpose and trust.

☑ Every leader can be a coach — by being more curious, present, and empowering.

"Leadership is not about giving answers — It's about creating spaces where others discover theirs."

Chapter 9

FROM AWARENESS TO LEGACY – THE CORPORATE ATHLETE'S EVOLUTION

Becoming the Change You Inspire in Others

"Greatness is not what you achieve when people are watching — it's what remains when you're gone."

The Journey Comes Full Circle

The Corporate Athlete's journey begins with *performance* and ends with *presence.*

You started as a **Player** — learning to perform with focus and discipline. You became a **Captain** — leading others with vision and courage. You evolved into a **Coach** — empowering others to grow.

And now, you stand at the next threshold — the path of the **Legacy Leader.**

This stage is about shifting from *achievement to awareness,* from *success to significance.* It's where leadership transcends metrics and becomes meaning in motion.

Anil Kumble: Legacy through Integrity

Anil Kumble wasn't the fastest bowler, nor the most celebrated, early in his career. But his legacy became larger than records — it became *values in action.*

When he bowled with a broken jaw against the West Indies in 2002, he wasn't proving toughness — he was demonstrating commitment. He didn't need to say a word; his action became a lesson for generations.

He once said:

"You don't play for applause. You play for pride."

That is legacy leadership — when what you stand for becomes larger than what you deliver.

Corporate Reflection:

In corporate life, integrity is the foundation of enduring impact. Your people won't remember every number you achieved, but they'll remember how you made decisions — especially when it was difficult.

Ask yourself:

"What do I want people to feel when they remember working with me?"

That's where legacy begins — in the emotional footprints you leave behind.

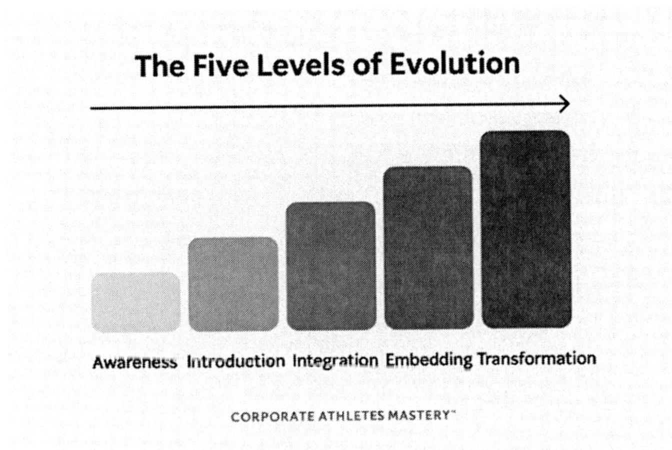

Figure 10: The Five Levels of Evolution

The Five Levels of Evolution™

Every leader, team, and organization evolves through five distinct levels. These are not just stages of performance — they're stages of *conscious leadership.*

Level 1 – Awareness

You can't change what you don't notice.

The journey begins when you start observing your patterns, habits, and reactions. You realize — performance is not just about doing, but about *being.* Awareness opens the door to growth.

Reflection: "What patterns define how I show up under pressure?"

Level 2 – Introduction

New habits meet old systems.

At this stage, you start applying what you've learned — creating space for coaching, feedback, and reflection in your work. The organization begins to *notice* a change. Resistance may surface — but persistence wins.

Reflection: "Where can I introduce coaching or mindfulness into my team rhythm?"

Level 3 – Integration

New habits become part of the workflow.

Now, the principles of performance, purpose, and coaching start blending into the organizational fabric. Meetings begin with reflection, not reporting. Managers listen more, teams self-correct faster.

Reflection: "How consistently am I living the principles I advocate?"

Level 4 – Embedding

Values turn into culture.

At this stage, coaching, reflection, and trust are no longer programs — they are practices. New leaders emerge naturally. Energy replaces exhaustion. Performance becomes sustainable.

Reflection: "What invisible habits define my team's culture today?"

Level 5 – Transformation

The culture becomes self-sustaining.

This is the level of **Legacy.** The organization doesn't depend on one leader — it thrives on shared leadership. Teams grow beyond processes. People don't just *work here* — they *become better humans here.*

Reflection: "What will continue to thrive here long after I've moved on?"

The Evolution Summary

Stage	Focus	Outcome
Awareness	Personal clarity	Reflection and responsibility
Introduction	Early adoption	Small visible changes
Integration	Consistency	Alignment between values and actions
Embedding	Sustainability	Culture of trust and reflection
Transformation	Legacy	Leadership that multiplies itself

This is how a Corporate Athlete evolves into a Legacy Leader.

The Art of Continuity: Playing the Long Game

Mithali Raj: Sustained Excellence

Mithali Raj, India's most successful women's cricket captain, never played for glory — she played for longevity. Her leadership wasn't loud; it was consistent, steady, and deeply purposeful.

Even in retirement, she continues to mentor, develop, and inspire younger athletes.

Her secret?

"I focused on process and people — results followed naturally."

Longevity is the mark of leadership maturity. It's not how fast you grow — it's how gracefully you sustain.

Corporate Reflection:

In corporate leadership, continuity comes from rhythm — balancing drive with downtime, strategy with reflection. When your growth system is consistent, your success becomes inevitable.

Ask yourself:

"What habits will keep me relevant for the next decade?"

Legacy leaders build systems that outlast circumstances.

The Legacy Loop™

Legacy is not the final stage — it's a continuous cycle of *evolution and renewal.* Every time one generation of leaders matures, another begins its journey.

This creates the **Legacy Loop™** — the sustainable cycle of leadership excellence.

Phase	Focus	Contribution
Learn	Discover principles, values, and practices	Build awareness
Lead	Apply and model behaviors	Inspire consistency
Coach	Multiply learning in others	Create ownership
Evolve	Reflect and refine	Renew purpose
Legacy	Pass on values and culture	Build continuity

Each loop feeds the next — ensuring that excellence is not dependent on individuals but driven by systems of reflection and trust.

"Legacy is not what you leave behind — it's what you leave within."

Sports Parallel – MS Dhoni: The Silent Legacy

MS Dhoni's greatest leadership act wasn't lifting the World Cup — it was *stepping aside* so a new leader could rise. His calm, detached approach redefined leadership for a new generation.

He showed that real leaders don't compete with successors — they *create* them.

That's the Corporate Athlete's ultimate purpose — to make themselves *unnecessary.*

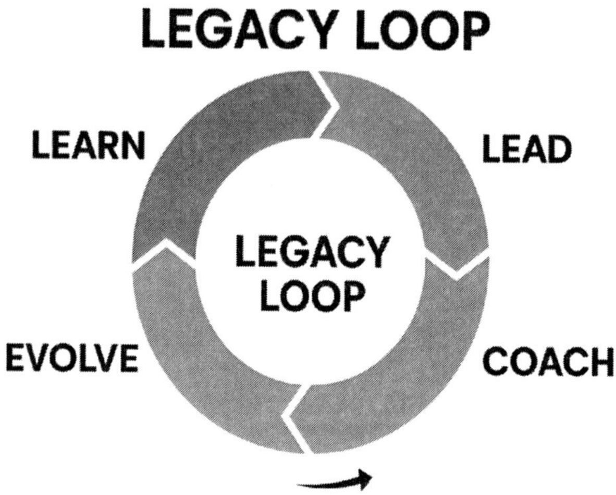

Figure 11: the Legacy Loop

Organizational Legacy: From Culture to Community

Great companies don't just deliver profits — they deliver purpose to people.

- **Infosys** institutionalized reflection through its Leadership Institute.
- **Biocon** focuses on ethics-driven innovation for the public good.
- **Tata Group** built its legacy on service, not scale.

In each case, legacy is not an artifact — it's a living mindset.

Organizations that evolve from *performance-driven* to *purpose-driven* become true ecosystems of excellence.

Corporate Reflection Exercise: The Legacy Canvas™

Draw five circles outward, like ripples on water. Label them:

Self → Team → Organization → Society → Future.

Now reflect:

- What am I contributing at each circle?
- What do I want each circle to remember about my leadership?

That's your personal legacy map.

The Transition from Legacy to Renewal

Every legacy, no matter how great, must evolve. The Corporate Athlete's journey never truly ends — it loops back to awareness, reflection, and renewal.

That's what keeps greatness alive — humility.

As Olympic legend Abhinav Bindra says:

"After the gold, I had to learn to live without the medal — to rediscover who I am beyond success."

Legacy leaders live with that awareness — they are not defined by what they've achieved, but by *what they continue to learn.*

Closing Reflection: Becoming the Evolution

Pause for a moment. Breathe. Reflect.

Ask yourself:

1. How far have I come — not in position, but in perspective?
2. What part of me still needs to evolve to serve more meaningfully?
3. What legacy am I already creating in others — through my presence, not my position?

Remember — legacy is not a destination. It's a living practice.

"The Corporate Athlete doesn't retire — they evolve."

KEY TAKEAWAYS

☑ Leadership maturity is the ability to evolve from success to significance.
☑ The Five Levels of Evolution™ map personal and cultural transformation.
☑ The Legacy Loop™ sustains excellence through reflection, renewal, and succession.
☑ Great leaders don't chase legacy — they *live* it daily.
☑ Your impact is measured not by what you control, but by what you inspire.

"The greatest legacy of a leader is not in their achievements, but in the awareness they awaken in others."

Chapter 10

THE CORPORATE ATHLETE MANIFESTO – FROM SURVIVE TO THRIVE TO DRIVE

Living the Inner Game of Performance, Purpose, and Presence

"You don't become a Corporate Athlete by what you achieve — you become one by how you show up every day."

The Journey So Far

The story of the Corporate Athlete began with a simple realization — that in the relentless pace of corporate life, survival is not enough.

We have to learn to thrive. And thriving is not just about speed — it's about *strength, stillness, and self-awareness.*

You began as the **Player**, mastering discipline and focus. You became the **Captain**, leading with vision and courage. You evolved into the **Coach**, empowering growth in others. You discovered **Purpose**, learned to play the **Infinite Game**, and began building your **Legacy**.

Now, as we conclude this journey, you are invited to live as a *Corporate Athlete* — Not just in what you do, but in *who you become every single day.*

From Survival to Self-Mastery

In the beginning, most professionals operate in **Survival Mode** — reactive, rushed, and relentlessly seeking control.

You manage deadlines, decisions, and demands — but somewhere, you lose depth.

The first step to mastery is awareness:

"I am more than my goals."

That's when you begin to shift — from reacting to responding, from control to consciousness.

This is where *self-leadership* is born — when you start managing your energy, not just your calendar.

Sports Parallel – Saina Nehwal's Comeback

After a major knee injury in 2016, Saina Nehwal could've quit. But she rebuilt herself, step by step, through patience, presence, and persistence. Her recovery was not just physical — it was mental and spiritual.

She once said:

"The biggest opponent is never across the net — it's the voice inside your head."

That's the essence of a Corporate Athlete — quieting the noise, centering the mind, and performing from clarity, not chaos.

Reflection:

Ask yourself:

- What's my biggest "injury" right now — burnout, self-doubt, fear of failure?
- How am I rebuilding my inner game?

Because healing, too, is a form of performance.

The Shift from Thrive to Drive

Once survival stabilizes, you begin to **Thrive** — performing with flow, clarity, and purpose. You learn to lead others with empathy and coach them with belief. You connect results with relationships.

But thriving is not the end — it's the *gateway to Drive.*

Drive is where purpose meets persistence — where your actions align so deeply with meaning that work feels like expression.

"When you stop chasing success and start serving purpose, excellence becomes effortless."

The 3-Stage Evolution Model

Stage	Mindset	Focus	Identity Shift
Survive	React	Efficiency	From control to clarity
Thrive	Respond	Effectiveness	From ego to empathy
Drive	Create	Excellence	From success to significance

This is the evolution every Corporate Athlete must make — again and again — throughout their journey.

Corporate Example – Biocon's Purpose-Driven Drive

Kiran Mazumdar-Shaw built Biocon not from ambition, but conviction — a belief that science must serve society.

In her own words:

"Purpose doesn't slow you down — it gives you the stamina to go further."

That's the kind of Drive that defines a Corporate Athlete — vision with compassion, success with service.

The Manifesto of the Corporate Athlete

This is your declaration — the code of mastery you live by.

THE CORPORATE ATHLETE MANIFESTO™

I am a Player — disciplined in effort, grounded in purpose. I train not to impress, but to improve. I play my game with integrity and intent.

I am a Captain — leading with courage and compassion. I serve the team, not the title. I build trust before I demand performance.

I am a Coach — I don't give answers; I create awareness. I believe in people until they believe in themselves. I measure success not by control, but by growth.

I am a Purpose Seeker — I don't chase meaning; I embody it. My work is an expression of my values. I don't compete to win — I compete to contribute.

I am a Legacy Builder — I lead so that others can lead. I leave not my achievements, but my awareness behind. I am part of something bigger than myself.

I am a Corporate Athlete — resilient in challenge, reflective in success, and renewed by purpose every single day.

Short Version for Reflection

"I am not defined by my role — I am refined by my reflection."

"My performance is my practice. My purpose is my peace. My presence is my power."

The 3 Rs of Corporate Athlete Mastery

To live the manifesto daily, practice the **3 Rs Framework™**:

Principle	Meaning	Application
Reflect	Awareness before action	Begin each day with mindful reflection.
Reframe	See differently to act wisely	When stressed, ask: "What else could this mean?"
Renew	Rest, recover, and realign	Protect your energy like a sacred asset.

These are not just habits — they are anchors. They keep you centered in a world of constant change.

Sports Parallel – Abhinav Bindra's Renewal

After winning Olympic gold, Abhinav Bindra went through depression and disillusionment. He later shared:

"I realized my biggest victory wasn't the medal — it was the mastery of myself."

Renewal is not a retreat from excellence — it's the *return to essence.*

The Five Practices of Everyday Mastery

1. **Morning Clarity:** Start each day by asking: "What truly matters today?"
2. **Energy Awareness:** Schedule recovery as seriously as meetings.

3. **Reflective Pauses:** Insert 2 minutes of silence before every big decision.
4. **Coaching Moments:** End meetings with one reflective question: "What did we learn today?"
5. **Gratitude Closure:** Finish your week by thanking one person — in writing, not thought.

These small rituals turn performance into a sacred practice.

Living the Legacy Loop™

Remember the Legacy Loop: **Learn → Lead → Coach → Evolve → Legacy.**

Now, embed it into your rhythm:

- **Learn** something new each week.
- **Lead** one person with empathy.
- **Coach** one colleague to reflect, not react.
- **Evolve** through feedback.
- **Leave** something better than you found it.

If you do that, every week becomes meaningful.

Closing Reflection: Your Infinite Game

The Corporate Athlete doesn't retire — they evolve. They don't wait for opportunity — they create it. They don't seek applause — they seek alignment.

And when their time comes to step aside, they leave behind not titles, but transformation.

"One day, people won't remember what you did — they'll remember how they felt because you were there."

That is legacy. That is leadership. That is mastery.

KEY TAKEAWAYS

☑ The Corporate Athlete evolves through three life stages: **Survive → Thrive → Drive.**

☑ Awareness, purpose, and reflection are the foundation of resilience.

☑ The Corporate Athlete Manifesto is a daily code of living — not just leading.

☑ Legacy is not about being remembered; it's about being reproduced in others.

☑ The infinite game is not about duration — it's about direction.

"When performance meets purpose, and purpose meets presence — mastery becomes who you are."

Figure 12: The Corporate Athlete Manifesto

EPILOGUE

The Spirit of the Corporate Athlete

Where Purpose Meets Presence

"There comes a moment in every journey when the pursuit turns inward. When the noise of achievement fades, and what remains is a quiet question — Who have I become through what I have done?"

That question marks the beginning of mastery. Because true excellence is not about *doing more* — it's about *being more.*

The Journey Within

You began this journey as the **Player** — learning the power of discipline, focus, and preparation. You discovered that performance isn't a stage; it's a *practice.*

Then you became the **Captain** — learning to lead with clarity and courage. You realized that leadership is not about authority, but *authenticity.*

Next, you evolved into the **Coach** — learning to grow others through awareness and belief. You understood that the best way to develop people is to *trust their potential.*

And eventually, you became the **Legacy Builder** — recognizing that your influence is not in what you control, but in what you *inspire.*

Through it all, one truth emerged — The Corporate Athlete's real competition is not the world outside, but the noise within.

Beyond Winning

In sports, victory lasts a moment — but values last a lifetime. Champions rise not from medals, but from mindsets.

Just as a cricketer learns to bat through failure, a corporate athlete learns to *lead through uncertainty.*

When a tennis player loses form, they don't quit — they go back to fundamentals. So must we — return to reflection, rhythm, and renewal.

You've learned that every burnout carries a lesson. Every setback hides a seed of strength. Every challenge is an invitation to return to purpose.

"The body performs. The mind strategizes. But it is the spirit that sustains."

The Stillness Within the Storm

In a world obsessed with urgency, the Corporate Athlete moves with rhythm. In a world crowded with voices, they lead with silence. In a world that measures success by speed, they measure it by *significance.*

They have learned that excellence is not a peak — it's a pattern. Not a finish line — but a way of showing up.

When you play your *outer game* with excellence and your *inner game* with grace — you transcend both pressure and praise.

Sports Parallel – Mary Kom's Spirit

Mary Kom, the six-time world champion boxer, embodies this spirit. Each time she fell, she rose stronger — not for fame, but for purpose. Her mantra:

"Don't let anyone tell you what you can't do. The ring is just a mirror — it shows you who you already are."

That's the spirit of a Corporate Athlete — resilient, humble, and aware that every round, every challenge, It is an opportunity to meet oneself anew.

The Inner Conversation

Pause for a moment.

Ask yourself:

- Have I been living in reaction or reflection?
- Do I chase goals, or do I *choose* growth?
- When was the last time I felt fully present in my work — not distracted, not divided, just *here*?

Presence is not the absence of action — it's the fullness of awareness within it.

When you act from presence, you bring your whole self — body, mind, and spirit — to every meeting, every challenge, every conversation. And that changes everything.

The Rhythm of Renewal

Just as athletes rest between matches, corporate athletes must rest between milestones.

Recovery is not weakness — it's wisdom.

You cannot pour from an empty cup. You cannot lead from an uncentered heart. You cannot inspire from exhaustion.

That's why the Corporate Athlete builds rituals of renewal — silence, stillness, gratitude, and reflection.

Because the *next season of greatness* always begins in *the pause.*

The Final Lesson: From Mastery to Meaning

Mastery is when performance and purpose merge. Meaning is when purpose and presence unite.

Together, they form the essence of the Corporate Athlete.

At this point, you realize — It was never about the medals, the metrics, or the milestones. It was about *the person you became on the journey.*

"Success is what the world gives you. Significance is what you give the world."

That's your legacy — and it lives in every life you've touched with empathy, integrity, and inspiration.

The Way of the Corporate Athlete™

A simple circle — continuous, alive, infinite. It represents the rhythm of this path:

Perform → Lead → Coach → Reflect → Renew → Repeat.

Each turn of the circle deepens awareness, not exhaustion. Each season of your journey becomes a new expression of mastery.

Final Reflection

When you look back one day, you may not remember every project, promotion, or presentation. But you will remember —

- The day you chose reflection over reaction.
- The person you coached instead of correcting.
- The moment you led with empathy, not ego.
- The peace you felt when purpose replaced pressure.

Those moments — quiet, human, and real — These are the true medals of a Corporate Athlete.

"You are your own Player — mastering the game. You are your own Captain — charting the course. You are your own Coach — shaping your mindset. And through it all, you are the Athlete of Awareness — playing not for applause, but for alignment."

"When you align purpose with performance, discipline with devotion, and achievement with awareness — you no longer chase excellence. You become it."

This book is not a conclusion — it's a continuation. A call to live your purpose every day, in small ways that ripple far.

To every reader, leader, and learner — thank you for walking this path. May you lead with awareness, coach with compassion, and play your infinite game with joy.

— Kishore Thakur

Executive Coach | Author, Corporate Athletes!

The Way of Corporate Athlete – Your Journey Continues

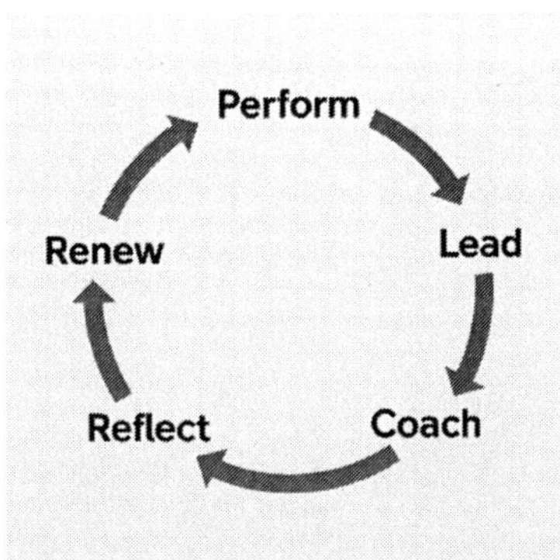

Figure 13: The way of Corporate Athlete

A continuous cycle of growth — from performance to purpose, from effort to excellence.

APPENDIX - REFLECTION JOURNAL PROMPTS

A Companion for the Corporate Athlete's Inner Journey

This Reflection Journal is designed to help you turn insight into practice — to pause, reflect, and realign with the rhythm of performance and purpose. You can revisit these prompts weekly, monthly, or at key transitions in your career. Use them not as checklists, but as conversations — with yourself.

🏁 Part I — The Arena of Performance

Chapter 1 – The New Game of Work

1. Where in my work do I perform continuously without recovery?
2. When was the last time I truly felt *in flow* — fully focused, energized, and present?
3. What one habit is quietly draining my energy every day?
4. How can I begin treating my work as a performance practice rather than a pressure cycle?

Chapter 2 – From Employee to Athlete

1. What patterns do I notice in my energy highs and lows through the week?
2. Which energy dimension (physical, emotional, mental, spiritual) needs most attention right now?
3. What micro-habit could help me recover faster between intense work cycles?
4. What does "thriving" — not just surviving — look like for me in my role?

⚡ Part II — The Leadership Within

Chapter 3 – The Player

1. How do I prepare before a high-stakes meeting or performance moment?
2. What routines help me stay consistent, regardless of pressure?
3. How do I measure progress — by effort, results, or learning?
4. Which area of my "practice" (discipline, focus, or reflection) deserves renewed attention?

Chapter 4 – The Captain

1. What does leadership mean to me — position, influence, or service?
2. How do I balance results with relationships in daily work?
3. When was the last time I made a courageous decision aligned with my values?
4. How can I build more trust through listening and empathy this week?

Chapter 5 – The Coach

1. When do I catch myself solving instead of coaching?
2. What kind of questions help people think for themselves?
3. How often do I pause and reflect before responding to a challenge?
4. What belief about people would make me a more empowering leader?

🧠 Part III — The Inner Game

Chapter 6 – Mindset, Resilience, and Renewal

1. How do I typically respond to setbacks — react, reflect, or reset?
2. What practices help me stay grounded under stress?
3. How do I build mental recovery into my routine?
4. What story do I tell myself about failure — and is it serving me?

Chapter 7 – Purpose and Peak Performance

1. What do I love doing so much that it feels effortless?
2. What strengths do I naturally bring to my work?
3. How does my work serve something larger than myself?
4. Where do my passion, skill, and purpose meet?

Part IV — From Culture to Legacy

Chapter 8 – Coaching in Action

1. What kind of conversations define my team culture — directive or reflective?
2. How can I make coaching a daily behavior, not a periodic activity?
3. Who in my circle could benefit from a "coaching moment" today?
4. What's one small question that could spark awareness in others?

Chapter 9 – From Awareness to Legacy

1. What impact do I want to create through my leadership?
2. What behaviors define the legacy I want to leave behind?
3. How am I modeling reflection and growth for those around me?
4. How will I continue my evolution from awareness to action?

Chapter 10 – The Corporate Athlete Manifesto

1. What does "Survive → Thrive → Drive" mean to me personally?
2. How can I renew my rhythm — physically, mentally, emotionally, and spiritually?
3. What does sustainable excellence look like in my daily routine?
4. How will I live the Corporate Athlete ethos — to Perform, Lead, Coach, Reflect, Renew, and Repeat?

Closing Reflection

- What has changed in how I see myself as a professional and as a person?
- What practices do I want to carry forward from this book into my daily life?
- If I were to write a one-line "Athlete's Creed" for my work, what would it say?

"Excellence begins when you start treating your work as a practice — not a race to win, but a rhythm to master."

REFERENCES AND INSPIRATIONS

Acknowledging the Thinkers, Teachers, and Trailblazers Who Shaped This Work

This book draws upon the collective wisdom of coaching science, leadership psychology, sports performance, and lived corporate experience. While the interpretations and integrations are entirely my own, the ideas have been inspired, informed, or reinforced by the following thinkers, frameworks, and movements.

---

1. Foundational Coaching Frameworks

- **International Coaching Federation (ICF)** — *Core Competencies, Code of Ethics, and Coaching Mindset Frameworks*
- **European Mentoring and Coaching Council (EMCC)** — *Global Competence Framework and Mentoring–Coaching Integration Principles*
- **Sir John Whitmore** — *"Coaching for Performance" and the GROW Model*
- **Julie Starr** — *"The Coaching Manual"*
- **David Clutterbuck** — *Mentoring and Developmental Coaching*
- **Nancy Kline** — *"Time to Think" and the concept of generative listening*

2. Leadership and Performance Science

- **Daniel Goleman** — *Emotional Intelligence* and the role of self-awareness in leadership
- **Jim Loehr & Tony Schwartz** — *"The Power of Full Engagement"* (energy management for peak performance)
- **Simon Sinek** — *"Start with Why"* and *"The Infinite Game"* (purpose-driven leadership)
- **Carol Dweck** — *Mindset: The New Psychology of Success* (growth vs. fixed mindset)
- **Stephen R. Covey** — *The 7 Habits of Highly Effective People* (personal mastery and alignment)
- **Adam Grant** — *Think Again* and *Give and Take* (rethinking assumptions and collaboration)

3. Sports and Human Performance Inspirations

- **Neeraj Chopra**, **P.V. Sindhu**, **M.S. Dhoni**, **Virat Kohli**, **Mary Kom**, **Rani Rampal**, and **Rahul Dravid** — for exemplifying resilience, preparation, humility, and leadership through action.
- **Gopichand Pullela** — for redefining coaching as a discipline of service and excellence.
- **Roger Federer**, **Novak Djokovic**, and **Serena Williams** — whose longevity and discipline embody the spirit of sustainable mastery.
- Principles from *sports psychology*, *Olympic mental conditioning*, and *elite coaching practices* that parallel corporate performance dynamics.

4. Organizational and Cultural Case Studies

- Public leadership and people development insights from:
    - **Tata Group** (values-based leadership and "Leaders as Coaches" philosophy)
    - **Infosys Leadership Institute** (coaching culture and reflective leadership)
    - **Google's Project Oxygen** (manager effectiveness and coaching behaviors)
    - **Microsoft's Growth Mindset transformation** (curiosity and learning culture)

(These references draw from published leadership insights, not internal data.)

---

5. Personal and Professional Learning Influences

- My clients, colleagues, mentors, and fellow coaches — whose experiences, reflections, and challenges inspired many stories in this book.
- Faculty and facilitators from coaching and leadership programs whose teaching reinforced that transformation begins with awareness.
- Countless athletes, leaders, and everyday professionals who reminded me that excellence is not about perfection — it's about preparation and presence.

6. Timeless Ideas and Wisdom Traditions

- Insights drawn from *Bhagavad Gita, Stoic philosophy (Marcus Aurelius)*, and *Zen mindfulness teachings* — emphasizing discipline, awareness, and purpose in action.
- Modern behavioral science research on *resilience, flow, and psychological safety* that underpin the "Corporate Athlete" approach.

Note from the Author

This book is a humble attempt to weave together lessons from sports, leadership, and coaching into a single fabric of practical wisdom. It stands not on originality of theory, but on authenticity of integration. Every concept here is a tribute to the teachers — seen and unseen — who have dedicated their lives to understanding how humans perform, lead, and grow.

"We all borrow light — the work is to pass it forward."

ABOUT THE AUTHOR

Kishore Kumar Thakur is an executive coach, leadership facilitator, and lifelong learner dedicated to helping professionals discover the deeper meaning behind performance, leadership, and growth.

With over two decades of experience in the corporate world, Kishore has worked with leaders across industries — guiding them to balance results with reflection, clarity with compassion, and ambition with awareness.

He believes that true success begins within — when professionals learn to lead themselves before leading others.

Drawing inspiration from coaching frameworks such as the **International Coaching Federation (ICF)** and the **European Mentoring and Coaching Council (EMCC)**, as well as timeless wisdom traditions, Kishore's work blends structure with soul, helping individuals and teams build sustainable excellence.

Through his writing, coaching, and workshops, he continues to inspire people to perform with purpose, lead with authenticity, and grow with grace.

Corporate Athletes! You are the Player, You are the Captain, You are the Coach is an invitation to every professional — to see work not just as a career, but as a journey of consciousness, contribution, and self-mastery.